Fw 200 CONDOR
VS
ATLANTIC CONVOY

1941–43

ROBERT FORCZYK

First published in Great Britain in 2010 by Osprey Publishing,
Midland House, West Way, Botley, Oxford, OX2 0PH, UK
44–02 23rd St, Suite 219, Long Island City, NY 11101, USA
E-mail: info@ospreypublishing.com

A CIP catalog record for this book is available from the British Library

Print ISBN: 978 1 84603 917 1
PDF e-book ISBN: 978 1 84908 265 5

Page layout by: Ken Vail Graphic Design, Cambridge
Index by Michael Forder
Typeset in ITC Conduit and Adobe Garamond
Maps and diagrams by bounford.com
Originated by PDQ Digital Media Solutions, Bungay, Suffolk
Printed in China through Bookbuilders

10 11 12 13 14   10 9 8 7 6 5 4 3 2 1

FOR A CATALOG OF ALL BOOKS PUBLISHED BY OSPREY
MILITARY AND AVIATION PLEASE CONTACT:

Osprey Direct, c/o Random House Distribution Center,
400 Hahn Road, Westminster, MD 21157
Email: uscustomerservice@ospreypublishing.com

Osprey Direct, The Book Service Ltd, Distribution Centre,
Colchester Road, Frating Green, Colchester, Essex, CO7 7DW
E-mail: customerservice@ospreypublishing.com

www.ospreypublishing.com

Acknowledgements
I would like to thank Nik Cornish, the staff at the Bundesarchiv,
the Imperial War Museum, John Cross at HITM Archives, the
US Library of Congress and the National Archives and Research
Administration for providing help with locating photographs and
other research materials. Also, Dr Geraldine Finlayson,
Co-Director of the Underwater Research Unit at the Gibraltar
Museum and Professor Dieter Scholz of Hamburg University of
Applied Sciences.

Dedication
This volume is dedicated to 1LT Jonathan P. Brostrom, C/2-503
Airborne Infantry Regiment, KIA 13 July 2008, Wanat,
Afghanistan.

Imperial War Museum Collections
Many of the photos in this book come from the Imperial War
Museum's huge collections which cover all aspects of conflict
involving Britain and the Commonwealth since the start of the
twentieth century. These rich resources are available online to
search, browse and buy. In addition to Collections Online, you can
visit the Visitor Rooms where you can explore over 8 million
photographs, thousands of hours of moving images, the largest
sound archive of its kind in the world, thousands of diaries and
letters written by people in wartime, and a huge reference library.
To make an appointment, call (020) 7416 5320, or e-mail
mail@iwm.org.uk.
Imperial War Museum www.iwm.org.uk

Artist's note
Readers may care to note that the original paintings from which
the color battlescene plates in this book were prepared are available
for private sale. All reproduction copyright whatsoever is retained
by the Publishers. All inquiries should be addressed to:

Howard Gerrard
11 Oaks Road
Tenterden
Kent
TN30 6RD
UK

The Publishers regret that they can enter into no correspondence
upon this matter.

CONTENTS

INTRODUCTION

After the fall of France in June 1940, the Third Reich was faced with only two strategic military options to deal with its remaining enemy, Great Britain. It could mount a direct assault on the home islands or it could adopt a blockade strategy and attempt to cut off the British economy from its overseas sources of raw materials. Adolf Hitler was never confident about mounting an invasion of Great Britain and even before the Luftwaffe made its bid to force the British to the negotiating table during the Battle of Britain, he authorized the Luftwaffe and Kriegsmarine to mount intensive attacks on British trade to bring their war economy to a standstill. While the Kriegsmarine had prepared for an attack on British trade routes with its U-boat arm, the Luftwaffe had not seriously considered long-range attacks on enemy shipping prior to 1940. However, in a remarkable display of ingenuity, and within a very short time, the Luftwaffe was able to adapt existing long-range Focke-Wulf Fw 200 Condor civil airliners to the anti-shipping mission and scored some impressive successes against Allied convoys that had little protection from air attack. Although not built for war, the Condor established such a combat reputation that Winston Churchill soon referred to it as "the scourge of the Atlantic."

In contrast, the Royal Navy spent considerable effort prior to the war on developing doctrine and tools for trade protection, but the main threats were thought to be U-boats and German surface raiders. Convoys, ASDIC and escorts were regarded as the answers to those threats. It was assumed that the Royal Air Force (RAF) would protect merchant shipping in British coastal waters from enemy air attack. Yet since very few long-range aircraft existed in the mid-1930s, the risk of air attack on convoys further out to sea was regarded as unlikely and few measures were taken to provide any kind of defense for this. Thus until mid-1941, the initial duel between the Luftwaffe's

Fw 200 Condors and Britain's Atlantic convoys was essentially one-sided, with merchant shipping virtually defenseless against air attack.

Yet in another amazing display of adaptability, the Royal Navy was able to develop a series of countermeasures in 1941–42, with some help from the RAF and United States Army Air Force (USAAF), that essentially neutralized the threat to shipping posed by the Fw 200 Condors. The development of Catapult Aircraft Merchant (CAM) ships and escort carriers, as well as better coordination with long-range aircraft of the RAF's Coastal Command, effectively created an air umbrella over the convoys that became increasingly difficult for the Condors to penetrate. Condors that attempted to bomb convoys were shot down with greater frequency and the Luftwaffe was forced to suspend this type of anti-shipping attack. However, just as it appeared that the duel had virtually been decided, the Luftwaffe added a new dimension in 1943 that offered the possibility of reversing the advantage once again, by introducing standoff attacks with guided missiles. It was only the general deterioration of the Luftwaffe's overall strength, and the growing power of Allied air forces, that prevented the missile-armed Condor and its successor, the Heinkel He 177, from inflicting serious losses on Allied convoys in 1943–44. In summary, the duel between Fw 200 Condors and Britain's Atlantic convoys illustrates the importance of being able to adapt off-the-shelf hardware for new missions, and highlights the difficulty of preventing a small enemy strike force from attacking shipping across a broad swath of ocean.

Pre-war postcard depicting an Fw 200 Condor airliner crossing the Atlantic. Focke-Wulf hoped to dominate the nascent trans-Atlantic passenger market with the Condor. This particular aircraft, one of the original pre-production models, was sold to Brazil in June 1939 and remained in service until 1947. (Author's collection)

CHRONOLOGY

1936
August 1   Lufthansa places order with Focke-Wulf for Fw 200 prototype.

1937
British Admiralty begins looking for new anti-aircraft (AA) weapon to equip merchant ships and escorts.

September 6   First flight of Fw 200 V1 prototype.

1938
June 27   An Fw 200 flies non-stop from Berlin to Cairo.

August 10   An Fw 200 achieves first non-stop flight from Berlin to New York City.

1939
March   Focke-Wulf begins converting an Fw 200 B into armed V10 prototype.

September 18   Luftwaffe orders 20 Fw 200 Cs for use as maritime patrol aircraft.

October 10   *Fernaufklärungsstaffel* is formed and soon re-designated 1./KG 40.

1940
February 19   KG 40 receives first Fw 200 C-1.

April 18   First Fw 200 attack on British shipping.

May 25   First Condor shot down by a British fighter.

June 9   First British merchant vessel sunk by KG 40 Condor.

July   Condors operate against individual shipping in the Western approaches

August 17   Germany declares a "total blockade" of Britain.

October 27   First Fw 200 attack on a convoy.

November 12   Admiralty and RAF agree to develop CAM ships.

1941
January 22   Royal Navy begins converting first escort carrier from merchant hull.

February 26   Convoy OB 290 is attacked by four Fw 200s, resulting in seven ships sunk.

Kurt Tank, the aeronautical engineer at Focke-Wulf GmbH. He was the driving force behind first developing the Fw 200 as a revolutionary civilian airliner and then converting it to a maritime patrol aircraft. Tank was eager to carve out military contracts for Focke-Wulf, which in 1939 was almost dead last among other German aircraft manufacturers in orders from the RLM. (Bundesarchiv, Bild 183-L18396)

The Fw 200 V-1 prototype approaching New York City on August 11, 1938. It had taken the Condor 24 hours and 36 minutes to fly the 6,371km (4,000 miles) from Berlin. This accomplishment was a major propaganda coup for Lufthansa, the Third Reich and Focke-Wulf GmbH. (Author's collection)

March 6	Churchill orders priority should be given to converting CAM ships.	**1942**	
May 5	RAF forms Merchant Ship Fighter Unit (MSFU).	**August**	CAM ships are discontinued in the Atlantic, but remain in the Mediterranean.
May 31	A CAM ship carries out first trial launch of a fighter.	**1943**	
June 20	HMS *Audacity*, first escort carrier, is commissioned.	**November**	III/KG 40 begins receiving Hs-293 guided bombs for its Condors.
August 3	A Hurricane from a Fighter Catapult Ship (FCS) shoots down an Fw 200 Condor.	**1944**	
September 21	A Martlet from HMS *Audacity* shoots down an Fw 200.	**February**	Fw 200 production ends.

DESIGN AND DEVELOPMENT

Fw 200 CONDOR

Once Hitler came to power in 1933, his regime was greatly interested in expanding the development of Germany's aviation industry and in conducting propaganda coups that would enhance the international prestige of the Third Reich. Whenever possible, these two policy goals were to be combined. The German national airline, Deutsche Lufthansa, offered excellent potential to develop such new dual-use technologies, both for future military applications as well as for shining a global spotlight on German technical prowess. The Reich Air Ministry (RLM) run by the former head of Lufthansa, Erhard Milch, was established to ensure close coordination between military and civil aviation.

Lufthansa was eager to carve out a dominant niche in the newly emerging commercial aviation market and in 1932 it had chosen the reliable Junkers-built Ju 52/3mce tri-motor as its standard passenger liner. By 1936, three-quarters of Lufthansa's 60-strong aircraft fleet were of this one type. Unfortunately, the Ju 52 could only compete economically on the medium-range routes to Spain, Italy and Scandinavia, and its lack of a pressurized cabin was hardly state-of-the-art in passenger comfort. When the American-built DC-2 appeared in 1934, followed by the even better DC-3 in 1935, Lufthansa's leadership knew that they needed a superior aircraft to the Ju 52 if they were going to compete for new long-haul routes to the Americas, Africa and the Far East. Developing a reliable means of transatlantic passenger service, which Lufthansa had been considering even before Hitler came to power, seemed a very attractive goal for German civil aviation. Initially, Lufthansa went with the "lighter-than-air" approach, constructing the airships *Graf Zeppelin* and *Hindenburg*. These airships were used to validate long-range navigation techniques, but their inherent fragility and huge cost marked them more as test beds rather than the final solution.

Once the DC-3 appeared, Lufthansa wanted a new civil airliner with intercontinental range that would allow it to dominate the new routes. The RLM also favored the development of long-range civilian airliners to compete with the new generation of American-built passenger planes, especially as Milch did not want the German aviation industry to fall behind foreign technological advances. With the RLM's blessing, Lufthansa began to approach the major German aircraft designers, but the two logical choices, Junkers and Dornier, proved less than helpful. Both companies were focused on developing bombers and winning large contracts from the Luftwaffe, rather than diverting scarce resources toward a small-scale civilian project. Although Junkers did agree to rebuild the prototype of its cancelled Ju 89 heavy bomber into a transport version known as the Ju 90, it would not initially commit itself to full-scale development. As a fallback Dr Rolf Stüssel, Lufthansa's technical chief, approached Focke-Wulf Flugzeugbau GmbH in Bremen about the possibility of developing a long-range multi-engined passenger airliner. Compared to Junkers and Dornier, Focke-Wulf had negligible experience in building such large, all-metal aircraft.

Focke-Wulf had enjoyed a close relationship with Lufthansa since the late 1920s, providing it with the Fw A17, Fw A32, Fw A33 and Fw A38 single-engined passenger planes. Although Focke-Wulf lacked experience designing large, multi-engined aircraft, it made up for this deficiency with a high level of motivation and a "can-do" attitude. In early July 1936, Stüssel and Lufthansa's director, Carl-August Freiherr von Gablenz,

ABOVE In order to achieve the Condor's remarkable 2400km (1,500-mile) combat radius, Kurt Tank had six 300-liter fuel tanks installed in the former passenger compartment. These tanks were highly vulnerable to any kind of tracer or incendiary bullets, which could quickly turn the interior of the Condor into a blazing torch. (Author's collection)

LEFT An Fw 200 C-3 photographed early in 1941, showing off its ventral gondola and C- and D-stand defensive stations. Hauptmann Fritz Fliegel was shot down in this aircraft on July 18, 1941, by flak from a merchant ship. (Bundesarchiv, Bild 146-1978-043-02)

Crew	6
Powerplant	4x 1,000hp-Bramo 323 R-2 supercharged radial engines[1]
Fuel	8,060 liters standard, 9,955 liters maximum
Weights	12,950kg (empty), 17,005kg (loaded)
Performance	
Maximum Take-off	24,520kg
Maximum Speed	360km/h (224mph) at 4,800m (15,750ft) 306km/h (190mph) at sea level
Cruise Speed	335km/h (208mph)
Ceiling	6,000m (19,685ft)
Range	3,560km (2,212 miles) with standard fuel 4,440km (2,760 miles) with maximum fuel
Armament	A-stand: 13mm MG 131 in turret B-stand: 13mm MG 131 rear-firing dorsal mount C-stand: 13mm MG 131 forward-firing in gondola D-stand: 7.92mm MG 15 rear-firing in gondola 2x Beam-mounted 13mm MG 131 4x SC-250 general purpose bombs or 2x SD-500 fragmentation bombs and 12x SD-50 bombs.
Cost	RM 273,500

[1] 1,200 hp with water-methanol injection

met with Kurt Tank to discuss Focke-Wulf's technical proposal for the new aircraft. Tank was an aeronautical engineer and test pilot who had been with Focke-Wulf for five years. As head of its technical department, he had recently designed the Fw 44 civilian biplane. Tank delivered an impressive presentation, convincing Stüssel and Gablenz that not only could Focke-Wulf design and build the new aircraft, but that a flying prototype could be ready within just one year. On August 1, 1936, Lufthansa signed an agreement with Focke-Wulf to develop an aircraft that could carry 25 passengers to a range of 1,500km (930 miles), which the RLM designated as the Fw 200.

Tank was eager to make a name for himself as an aeronautical designer and he took to the new project with relish. The Focke-Wulf design team, led by Dr Wilhelm Bansemir, quickly sketched a layout for the all-metal aircraft and Tank began to procure off-the-shelf components such as American-built Pratt & Whitney S1E-G Hornet radial engines, although the production aircraft would actually use BMW 132 engines. Amazingly, Tank accomplished this feat on schedule, with the V1 prototype being designed and assembled within 12 months. Even before Tank took the V1 on its inaugural flight on September 6, 1937, Lufthansa's leadership was so impressed that they pledged to order two more prototypes as well as three production aircraft. The airline kept its options open, however, and also showed interest in the larger Ju 90 passenger plane that made its first flight soon after the V1.

Although Tank was keen to show off the prototype, which was named "Condor," it took another year of further refinements before it was ready for long-distance flights. By the summer of 1938, Focke-Wulf and the RLM agreed to use the V1 prototype on a propaganda tour that would highlight the range and speed of the new aircraft.

Fw 200 C3/U4

6.29m (20.67ft)

32.85m (107.78ft)

23.45m (76.94ft)

In June 1938, Kurt Tank flew the prototype from Berlin to Cairo with 21 passengers on board. On August 10, 1938, a selected crew flew the prototype non-stop from Berlin to New York, a distance of 6,371km (4,000 miles), in just under 25 hours. Few of the reporters who witnessed this historic event noticed that the Condor's faulty brake system caused damage to its landing gear. Having set the transatlantic record, the prototype was sent on a round-the-world flight via Basra, Karachi, Hanoi and Tokyo, in November 1938. Emperor Hirohito of Japan personally met the crew and the Japanese were very impressed by the V1. However, when continuing on to Manila, the crew made a mistake with the fuel pumping system that caused the aircraft to ditch offshore. Despite the loss of the prototype and indications that this finicky aircraft was quite fragile, Tank had impressed the world with his Condor.

Converting this technological marvel into a profitable airliner proved to be more difficult than Lufthansa had realized. Since an Fw 200 cost almost three times as much as a Ju 52, the airline decided to order only three of them in 1938 and four more in 1939. The Condors were used on trial flights to Brazil and West Africa in 1939, further demonstrating the long-range capabilities of the aircraft, but these flights served more as a propaganda stunt than as a demonstration of the viability of a commercial passenger service. In order to keep the production line open and hopefully recoup its development costs, Focke-Wulf sought to export the Condor and sold two planes each to Denmark, Finland and Brazil. Two more were sold to the Luftwaffe to provide VIP transport for Hitler and other high-ranking Nazis, and in early 1939, the Japanese airline *Dai Nippon Kabushiki Kaisha* ordered a further five. The Imperial Japanese Navy was also interested in using the Condor as a maritime patrol bomber and asked Focke-Wulf to develop a military version. In March 1939, Focke-Wulf introduced the Fw 200 B as the standard production version and Tank selected the Fw 200 V10 (named "Hessen") – which was the prototype for the new B-series model – as the basis for a militarized version of the Condor to meet the Japanese requirement. The V10 was equipped with cameras and five light machine guns but had no provision for carrying bombs. However, before the V10 was even ready, World War II broke out in September 1939. Lufthansa was forced to suspend most of its long-distance international flights, but kept a few civilian Condors serving the routes to Rome, Madrid and Stockholm. Six of the existing Condors were handed over to the Luftwaffe's 4.*Staffel* of KGrzbV 105 for use as transports.

Although British Intelligence was convinced that the Luftwaffe was using Lufthansa as a test bed to covertly develop long-range bombers, the Luftwaffe leadership had no interest in the Fw 200 as a military aircraft prior to World War II. The Luftwaffe had begun developing the Do 19 and Ju 89 four-engined heavy bombers in 1936, but as they proved to be too expensive, both these projects were cancelled after just a few prototypes had been built. Subsequently the Luftwaffe leadership saw the Ju 86B passenger airliner as having potential use as a bomber and encouraged Lufthansa to order five of them. The Fw 200, however, was considered to be more a propaganda device than a potential weapon. Not expecting an imminent outbreak of war, the RLM had placed an order with Heinkel in early 1938 for the He 177, believing this would provide a long-range bomber for the Luftwaffe. The He 177 could carry 1,000kg of bombs over a distance of 6,695km (4,160 miles), which far exceeded the capabilities of militarized versions of civilian airliners. Yet the aircraft would not make its first flight until November 1939 and would not be ready for operational use until 1941–42 at best.

Just before war broke out, the Luftwaffe realized that it needed some kind of offensive anti-shipping capability in case of hostilities with Great Britain, and Generalleutnant Hans Geisler, a former officer in the Imperial Navy, was ordered to begin

forming the cadre of a new special-purpose unit. By pre-war agreement, the Kriegsmarine had no strike aircraft of its own and the Luftwaffe had been responsible for anti-shipping attacks. Once war began, Geisler's embryonic unit was organized as the X.*Fliegerkorps* and it was tasked with attacking British warships and merchant ships in the North Sea. At first, Geisler had three bomber groups with medium-range He 111s and Ju 88s, but he had no long-range aircraft. Since the He 177 bomber would not be ready for some time, Geisler ordered one of his staff officers, Hauptmann Edgar Petersen, to examine existing civilian airliners and determine if any would be suitable for use as auxiliary maritime patrol aircraft. Petersen initially looked at the Ju 90 passenger airliner, but only two had been completed before Junkers suspended the program. On September 5, 1939, Petersen went to the Focke-Wulf plant and met with Kurt Tank. Once again energetic in promoting his design, Tank convinced Petersen that the six nearly completed Fw 200 Bs intended for Japan could be converted into armed maritime patrol aircraft in just eight weeks and that more could be built in a matter of months. Petersen wrote a memorandum after his visit to Focke-Wulf, recommending that X.*Fliegerkorps* use armed Condors for both maritime reconnaissance and attacks on lone vessels. Generalmajor Hans Jeschonnek, Chief of the Luftwaffe's *Generalstab*, was reluctant to waste scarce resources on fielding an experimental unit with jury-rigged bombers, but General der Flieger Albert Kesselring, commander of *Luftflotte* 1, thought the concept was interesting and passed it on to Hitler. Petersen then found himself invited to Obersalzberg, where Hitler heard his briefing on the Fw 200 and gave approval to set up the new unit. With the Führer's blessing, the Luftwaffe High Command sanctioned Petersen's plan on September 18, 1939, and agreed to purchase the six nearly completed Fw 200 Bs intended for Japan, along with the two earmarked for Finland, and convert them into armed Fw 200 C-0 models. Even though the civilian version of the Fw 200 was priced at more than 300,000 Reichsmarks, Kurt Tank was so desperate to land a contract with the Luftwaffe that he sold these first aircraft to the RLM for only about 280,000RM each. Indeed, in 1939 Focke-Wulf only sold these eight Condors and six Fw 189 reconnaissance planes to the Luftwaffe, compared to the hundreds of aircraft sold by Dornier, Junkers, and Heinkel. Jeschonnek also remained ambivalent about how the Fw 200 C should be used and Petersen was initially authorized to form them into a *Fernaufklärungstaffel* (long-range reconnaissance squadron), not an anti-shipping unit.

Although some sources identify the V10 prototype as the genesis of the armed Condor, it was only equipped with defensive armament. In order to meet the X.*Fliegerkorps'* requirement for a reconnaissance bomber, Tank had to provide the Condor with the ability to both carry and accurately deliver bombs. This was no easy task since in contrast to purpose-built bombers, the Condor did not have either a bomb bay or a glazed nose for the bombardier. Starting with a standard Fw 200 B, which was redesignated V11, Tank added a ventral gondola beneath the fuselage, which could carry a simple bombsight and two light machine guns. Rather than try to fit bombs internally, Tank installed hardpoints under the wings and outboard engine nacelles to carry a total of four 250kg bombs. He also added a small dorsal turret (A-stand) behind the cockpit and another dorsal MG 15 position (B-stand) further aft. By removing all the seats from the passenger area and replacing them with internal fuel tanks, he increased fuel capacity by 60 percent, which resulted in a combat radius of about 1,500km. Overall weight of the aircraft was increased by about two tons, but Tank was in such a hurry to deliver the Fw 200 C-0 to the Luftwaffe that he failed to strengthen the structure or examine the impact of carrying bombs and a heavy fuel load. The Fw 200 C-0 was also significantly slower than the civilian passenger version. Once completed in December 1939, the V11 was standardized as the Fw 200 C-1, which the Luftwaffe initially designated as the "Kurier" to differentiate it from Condor civilian models.

On October 10, 1939, Hauptmann Petersen took command of the *Fernaufklärungstaffel* at Bremen. This *staffel*, which was redesignated as 1./KG 40 in November, trained on unarmed Condor transports until the first Fw 200 C models began to arrive in February 1940. The RLM waited until March 4, 1940, to sign a series production contract with Focke-Wulf, which specified the construction of 38 Fw 200 C-1 and C-2 models for a fixed price of 273,500RM each, minus weapons. At that point, Focke-Wulf began serial production of the Fw 200 at the rate of four aircraft per month, a situation which remained in effect until 1942.

By the start of the invasion of Norway in April 1940, Petersen had a handful of operational Fw 200 C-0 and C-1s, which he used to conduct long-range reconnaissance missions around Narvik and to harass British shipping. Although Petersen's unit was able to sink only one British merchant ship during the Norwegian Campaign, some of the limitations of the Fw 200 were now realized and valuable experience was gained. Most of the pre-production Fw 200 C-0s that Tank had built so quickly suffered from cracks in their fuselage and wings, caused by the problems of overloading and a landing gear that could not handle rough airstrips. Furthermore, the defensive armament was quite weak and the lack of armor plate and self-sealing fuel tanks made the Fw 200 extremely vulnerable to even light damage. On May 25, 1940, a British Gloster Gladiator pilot intercepted one of KG 40's Fw 200 C-1s over Norway and was amazed to see the aircraft crash after a brief burst of .303in machine gun fire. Petersen remained convinced as to the potential of the Fw 200, but recommended that Focke-Wulf quickly develop more robust and better-armed Condors in order to carry the fight to the British at sea. Kurt Tank spent the next three years trying to upgrade the Condor, increasing its range, armament and protection, but was never able to escape the fact that the basic design was poorly suited for a demanding combat environment.

BRITISH SHIPBOARD ANTI-AIRCRAFT DEFENSES

Throughout the 1930s, the Royal Navy relied primarily on three weapons to provide layered shipboard air defense: the 12-pdr (76.2mm) QF and quad 2-pdr (40mm) cannon, and the quad .50in (12.7mm) Mk III machine gun. The 12-pdr had entered Royal Navy service back in 1913 as its first purpose-built AA gun, but it was a manually operated weapon with a low rate of fire. The quad 2-pdr, known as the "pom-pom," had entered service in 1930 and the Royal Navy placed great faith in its barrage fire capabilities of 400–450 rounds per minute (rpm) per mount. However, in combat the "pom-pom" tended to jam frequently and its rate of fire proved to be inadequate. At the low end of the spectrum, the .50in heavy anti-aircraft machine gun (AAMG) introduced in 1926 proved even more disappointing. In theory, the 12-pdrs would provide the outer air defense ring out to 7,000m with a rate of fire of 12–14rpm per mount, while the "pom-poms" provided the middle ring out to 4,000m and the AAMGs provided point defence out to about 700m. Pre-war estimates suggested that perhaps ten percent of the rounds fired might hit an approaching aircraft, so the Royal Navy was satisfied with installing just one AA gun mount on most of its escorts. However, British pre-war anti-aircraft tactics relied on the obsolete method of curtain fire – massing fire in a barrier between the ship and aircraft – rather than trying to actually strike the incoming aircraft. In reality, existing gun direction systems on British ships were incapable of tracking fast-moving targets at low level and the handful of AA guns on British escorts could not mass sufficient fire to protect a convoy that might stretch for miles.

The Admiralty was aware that its anti-aircraft defenses were falling behind developments in aviation technology and in 1937 it began to look for a new weapon that could be used specifically on small escort warships and merchant ships. The Swiss firm Oerlikon had developed a 20mm anti-aircraft gun that seemed promising, but

BELOW LEFT
A gun crew on a British trawler practices loading a 12-pounder AA gun in 1940. This elderly weapon had far too low a rate of fire to effectively deter low-level aircraft attacks. Note the dog next to the gun crew. (Imperial War Museum A 17177)

BELOW RIGHT
A twin 40mm Bofors AA gun firing aboard the escort carrier HMS *Tracker* in September 1943. *Tracker* escorted several convoys on the Halifax-to-Liverpool run in late 1943, and in March 1944 its fighters would shoot down three Condors. (Imperial War Museum A 19749)

The Royal Navy set up several courses to teach merchant sailors how to use elderly weapons like these Lewis and Hotchkiss machine guns for anti-aircraft defense of their ships. Britain had more than 50,000 of these weapons in stock and oftentimes these were the only shipboard defense against Condor attacks in 1940–41. (Imperial War Museum A 5227)

the Royal Navy initially rejected it as too complicated and expensive to manufacture. It was not until after war broke out in September 1939 that the Admiralty changed its mind and ordered a prototype from Oerlikon. About 100 Oerlikon guns were purchased before the fall of France in June 1940 cut off all further imports from Switzerland. The British succeeded in getting the design for the weapon, but failed to assign it high priority so production did not begin in Britain until November 1941. Eventually, the 20mm Oerlikon proved to be an excellent AA weapon, providing three times the rate of fire of the "pom-pom" out to 4,000m, and it was extremely effective against low-level air attacks. Very few Oerlikons were at sea during the critical period of 1940–41 however, and the Navy allocated the majority to defense of the fleet rather than defense of convoys. Another excellent foreign-built AA weapon that emerged just before the outbreak of war was the Swedish 40mm Bofors. Although the British Army adopted it, the Royal Navy was slow to recognize that it outclassed the "pom-pom" and it did not enter naval service until late 1941. As with the Oerlikon, the Bofors went to arm capital ships first and did not begin to reach escorts or merchant ships until 1942–43.

At the outbreak of war, the British Admiralty knew it would not have enough escorts to adequately protect every convoy, so the Royal Navy developed the Defensively Equipped Merchant Ships (DEMS) program. This would provide surplus naval armament to civilian vessels to protect themselves against both U-boat and air attack. As originally envisaged, the DEMS program recommended equipping each British merchant ship with one low-angle medium-caliber gun (between 76mm and 152mm), one 12-pdr anti-aircraft gun and one or more AAMGs. However, given that there were more than 1,900 ocean-going vessels in the British Mercantile Marine and just 877 of the 12-pdr guns in naval stocks, DEMS lacked the resources to arm even half the merchant fleet to minimum standard. Exacerbating the weapon shortage, the Royal Navy decided to requisition 54 civilian vessels at the outset of the war for conversion into Armed Merchant Cruisers (AMCs), each armed with six to eight 152mm guns and two 12-pdr AA guns. The Admiralty concentrated its efforts through the winter months of 1939–40 on equipping these AMCs, which were primarily intended for defense against surfaced U-boats and surface raiders. As a result, fielding the AMCs diverted a large number of weapons and trained gun crews into vessels that generally proved ill suited as convoy escorts.

Throughout the "Phony War" period, as less than one percent of the merchant tonnage lost was sunk by air attacks and limited to the North Sea area, the Admiralty continued to focus on defense against surfaced U-boats and commerce raiders. The Royal Navy trained some merchant sailors to act as gun crews and provided naval personnel to form cadres on larger civilian vessels, but prioritizing the AMCs delayed any significant improvements in merchant ship defenses until well into 1940. In March and April 1940, only 17 merchant vessels were armed under DEMS and 25 were provided with Lewis guns. However when France fell abruptly in June 1940, British merchant convoys suddenly began to come under low-level Luftwaffe air attack, not just in coastal waters but even to the west of Ireland, and very few vessels had any kind of defense against them. Even if a convoy had an escorting destroyer or sloop, such vessels' AA weapons proved barely capable of defending themselves, never mind a convoy of 20–30 ships spread out over a large area.

In desperation, the Admiralty sought *ad hoc* measures to accelerate the DEMS program and provide some degree of self-protection against air attack for every ship in a convoy. The Admiralty asked the British Army for help and 250 two-man light machine gun teams were provided by the Maritime Royal Artillery (MRA) Regiment for service aboard merchant ships. By the start of the Condor attacks against individual ships in July 1940, most merchantmen were fortunate if they had an elderly Lewis or Hotchkiss light machine gun, even though these weapons offered little chance of shooting down a fast-moving target. The Admiralty strengthened DEMS by establishing a special school for teaching anti-aircraft gunnery to merchant sailors, and added more Royal Navy sailors and Royal Marines to act as gun crews on convoys. The British Army also expanded its commitment by forming the Maritime Anti-Aircraft Regiment, Royal Artillery, in 1941, which it placed under Royal Navy command. The Royal Canadian Navy also made great efforts to improve training for merchant gun crews, but most of these efforts would not begin to pay off until late 1941 or early 1942.

Aggravating the problems caused by the dearth of effective anti-aircraft weapons, trained gun crews and appropriate tactics, the air defense of British convoys was seriously undermined by the lack of adequate early warning of enemy air attack. The Royal Navy had given little priority to developing air surveillance radar before the war and had only installed an experimental set on a minesweeper in early 1938. By the outbreak of war, the Admiralty had standardized the Type 79Y air surveillance radar, but it was only fitted on the battleship HMS *Rodney* and cruisers HMS *Sheffield* and HMS *Curlew*. An order was placed to equip 38 more ships, but then only battleships and cruisers, as the emphasis was placed on fleet, not convoy, defense. The Royal Navy slowed down the introduction of radar into the fleet by mandating that only new-build ships or ships in long-term repair would receive the Type 79Y, which ensured that few vessels were equipped before mid-1941. Even if a convoy was given a cruiser escort, the

THE 20MM OERLIKON

The rescue tugboat HMS Seaman (W-44) was the first vessel to shoot down a Condor with a 20mm Oerlikon gun on 10 January 1941. Although the Oerlikon's effective range was 2,000m (6,562ft), against a low-flying aircraft approaching at 290km/h (180mph), the gunner would begin firing at about 685m (2,250ft) as it filled the inner ring of the foresight. He would then only have about seven seconds before the Condor was within bombing range. The Oerlikon had a 60-round drum full of HE-T or HEI-T ammunition and the tracer rounds gave the gunner a good ability to determine if he was actually hitting the target.

The Condor comes into range around 685m out

The gunner opens fire with tracer rounds

Type 79Y had a fairly narrow beam and could only detect aircraft flying at just over 6,000m (19,200ft) out to 150km (95 miles). Throughout most of 1940–41, Allied convoys had little or no radar warning of low-level Condor attacks. It was not until the introduction of the improved Type 271 and Type 281 radar in late 1941 that smaller warships began to receive some form of early warning, and by 1942 even the ubiquitous Flower class corvettes were receiving radar. Once the convoy escorts were adequately equipped with radar in 1942–43, the Condors lost their main advantage of surprise.

BRITISH EFFORTS TO PROVIDE AIR COVER FOR CONVOYS

The Admiralty had first studied the idea of converting merchant ships into auxiliary aircraft carriers (AVGs) for trade protection in 1937–38, but the proposal was shelved due to lack of funding. However once war began, it quickly became obvious that the RAF would not be able to protect distant convoys at sea from air attack and that shipboard defenses were inadequate. In particular, the long-range Fw 200 Condors were able to strike convoys with near-impunity in areas well beyond range of land-based RAF fighters. At an inter-service conference on November 12, 1940, First Sea Lord Admiral Sir Dudley Pound and Air Chief Marshal Sir Charles Portal discussed

A Short Sunderland Mk I from Coastal Command's 210 Squadron flying a convoy escort mission over the Atlantic on 31 July 31, 1940. The Germans dubbed the Sunderland "the Flying Porcupine" because of its potent .50cal machine gun turrets and robust construction, which made it a tough adversary when encountered by the Fw 200s over the Atlantic. (Imperial War Museum CH 805)

a number of possible emergency measures for deterring Condor attacks, including the use of expendable aircraft launched from merchant ships. Captain Matthew S. Slattery, director of the Admiralty's Air Materiel Department, proposed two basic methods of providing expedient air cover for convoys: "the fitting of catapults to suitable merchant ships" and "the fitting of the simplest possible flight decks and landing equipment to suitable merchant ships." Pound decided to employ both methods and authorized the Royal Navy to find appropriate merchant vessels to convert, while Portal offered 60 older Hurricane fighters for use on the catapult ships. The ability of the British services to cooperate, unlike the Germans, was decisive in their eventual success in the duel between Condors and convoys.

Unfortunately, there were very few surplus catapults to hand and the existing cordite-powered model was designed to launch a floatplane at speeds up to 95km/h (60mph), whereas the Hurricane fighter required a speed of at least 125km/h (80mph)

A Hurricane Mk IA fighter mounted on the 23m (75ft) rocket catapult on the CAM ship SS *Empire Tide*. Hurricanes were loaded onto the ship using cranes, and each CAM ship had two fighters, with one ready to launch and the other on deck. (Author's collection)

A Hurricane pilot would have to climb a 9m (30ft) ladder in order to reach the Hurricane's cockpit, and then he would sit in the cockpit for a two-hour shift. The catapult was angled toward the starboard bow and the fighter sat atop a trolley that was propelled forward by a series of 3-inch rockets. (Author's collection)

to get into the air. The Royal Navy mounted cordite-powered catapults on the auxiliary ships HMS *Pegasus* and HMS *Springbank*, which became the first of the Fighter Catapult Ships (FCSs). Instead of using the higher-performance Hurricane fighter, these two ships carried one Fairey Fulmar fighter each, which were the absolute weight limit that the catapults could launch. *Pegasus* was converted quickly in December 1940, but *Springbank* was not ready until May 1941. Nevertheless, the Admiralty realized that it needed a better launching mechanism and tasked the research unit at the Royal Aircraft Establishment at Farnborough with developing an alternative. In a remarkable piece of wartime improvisation, the engineers at Farnborough built a prototype rocket catapult that could launch a Hurricane from a 23m (75ft) rail. The Hurricane was mounted on a trolley atop a twin rail launcher and was catapulted by the force of 13 electrically fired 3in rockets. This was an extremely dangerous method of launching a fighter, and it only allowed for a single launch since there was nowhere for the pilot to land after his sortie. Instead, the pilot would have to ditch near a rescue ship and hope for the best. The Farnborough engineers wanted more time to perfect the rocket catapult but Churchill became personally involved and demanded that it be fielded as soon as possible. On March 6, 1941, he ordered that: "extreme priority will be given to fitting out ships to catapult or otherwise launch fighter aircraft against bombers attacking our shipping."

The Royal Navy converted three more auxiliaries into FCSs in the spring of 1941 and equipped them with the new rocket-powered catapults and Hurricane fighters. However, the main effort went into converting a large number of civilian vessels into Catapult Aircraft Merchant (CAM) ships. Churchill initially demanded the conversion of 250 vessels into the CAM configuration but the Royal Navy reduced this to a more realistic 50. The first CAM ship, the *Michael E.*, was ready by May 28, 1941, and eventually 35 merchant vessels were converted. The RAF formed the Merchant Ship Fighter Unit (MSFU) near Liverpool on May 5, 1941, to provide a small detachment for each CAM ship, but the remaining crew members were merchant seamen. Each CAM ship was also given a radar set in order to provide sufficient time to prepare the flight for launch. By the summer of 1941 there were enough FCS and CAM ships to accompany some

A Lockheed Hudson Mk V of Coastal Command's 48 Squadron on patrol in 1942. The Hudson had only a slight speed advantage over the Condor and its four .303cal machine guns were inferior to the Fw 200 C-3's armament. (Imperial War Museum COL 183)

The CAM ship *Empire Spray* with a convoy on 22 October 22, 1941. CAM ships were usually deployed near the front of the convoy and by this time it was not uncommon to have two such ships in each convoy that was threatened by Condor attack. (Imperial War Museum C 4050)

of the convoys at greatest risk of Condor attack, but since the ships carried only one fighter apiece, each could only provide a single sortie over a convoy. Lack of continual coverage was the weakness of the catapult fighter concept. Nonetheless, the deployment of Hurricane fighters on FCS and CAM ships in mid-Atlantic surprised the *Kampfflieger* from KG 40 and began exacting a toll on the Condors by August 1941.

Although the Admiralty complied with Churchill's insistence on fielding the CAM ships, it also began a longer-term effort to develop ships that could carry several aircraft and use them more than once. The Royal Navy wanted an auxiliary carrier about half the size of a fleet carrier that could be built in 12–15 months. The first tentative step was taken in January 1941 when the Admiralty ordered the conversion of the captured German cargo ship *Hanover* (5,500 Imperial tons) into the auxiliary carrier[1] HMS *Audacity*. The superstructure was removed and the ship was given a flight deck, but it had no catapult, elevators, or "island," and the aircraft were stored on deck, exposed to the elements at all times. *Audacity* was commissioned in June 1941 and embarked 802 Squadron of the Fleet Air Arm (FAA) with six Grumman Martlet (F4F) fighters. Although very crudely built, *Audacity* quickly proved its worth in three months of intense combat while escorting convoys to Gibraltar, and its fighters shot down four Condors. Impressed by the success of *Audacity*, the Royal Navy decided to improve upon this prototype by developing two new classes of escort carrier. However, as British yards were fully committed to existing warship and merchant ship construction and had no spare capacity, the Admiralty decided to purchase merchant hulls from the still neutral United States. Four ships of the Archer class and 11 ships of the Attacker class were ordered from American yards. Unlike *Audacity*, these carriers were fitted with elevators and hydraulic catapults and could operate 15–20 embarked aircraft. The first of these improved escort carriers, HMS *Biter*, became operational in June 1942, followed by three more before the end of the year and 14 more in 1943. Thus, the British went from a position of non-existent mid-Atlantic air cover over convoys in 1939–40, to sporadic cover in 1941–42, and robust air cover by 1943.

[1] The Royal Navy initially designated these ships as Auxiliary Aircraft Carriers (AVGs) but reclassified them as Escort Carriers (CVEs) in 1942.

ATLANTIC CONVOY AIR COVER

Sea Hurricane IA V6802/LU-B, flown by Pilot Officer A S C Lumsden, Merchant Ship Fighter Unit, MV *Daghestan*, North Atlantic, September–October 1941

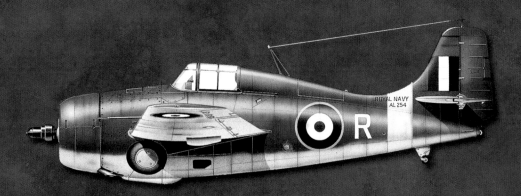

Grumman Martlet I AL254/R, flown by Sub-Lieutenant Eric Brown, 802 Squadron, Fleet Air Arm, HMS *Audacity*, November 8, 1941

HMS *Audacity*, commissioned June 1941, carrying 802 Squadron, Fleet Air Arm

RAF COASTAL COMMAND AND USAAF

The RAF's Coastal Command was assigned the mission of protecting Britain's merchant convoys from attacks by U-boats and Condors. Unfortunately it lacked the training, tactics, and proper aircraft to pose a serious threat to Condor anti-shipping operations until 1942. At the time that Condors began their attacks in July 1940, Coastal Command's No. 15 Group had been responsible for patrolling the Southwest Approaches and providing convoy escorts. However, No. 15 Group only had about 60 aircraft for this mission, consisting of Short Sunderland flying boats, Lockheed Hudson and Armstrong-Whitworth Whitley V bombers, and obsolete Avro Ansons. None of these aircraft were ideal for intercepting the Condor since they were all slow and lightly armed, lacking the range to cover the entire sea zone threatened by Fw 200 strikes. Typically, No. 15 Group would dispatch one or two aircraft to escort each convoy as it approached England and they would patrol around the ships for a few hours to deter Condor attacks. Given this sporadic air umbrella, air-to-air combats between Coastal Command aircraft and Fw 200s were rare in 1940–41, but of the five actions recorded, two resulted in RAF aircraft lost (one Hudson and one Whitley) versus two Condors destroyed and one damaged. The Sunderland, known as "the Flying Porcupine," had sufficient endurance to stay with a convoy and heavy enough armament to drive off an Fw 200, but lacked the speed to pursue and finish off damaged aircraft.

Coastal Command finally gained an aircraft that had a reasonable chance of intercepting a Condor with the introduction of the Beaufighter Mk IC long-range heavy fighter in April 1941. Armed with four 20mm cannon in its nose and over 160km/h (100mph) faster than the Fw 200, the Beaufighter proved to be a potent threat when one shot down a Condor on April 16, 1941. Although the Condors generally shied away from the few convoys protected by Beaufighters, this became less possible as Coastal Command fielded long-range fighters in greater numbers. Beaufighters shot down one Fw 200 in 1941, damaged two more in 1942, and shot down five in 1943. During July and August 1943, Coastal Command was also assisted in convoy protection by the USAAF 480th Anti-Submarine Group's B-24D Liberator bombers, which shot down a further four Condors. In December 1943, Coastal Command began using the De Havilland Mosquito fighter-bomber over the Bay of Biscay, which effectively made Condor operations in the Western Approaches suicidal.

An Fw 200 C-3 on a maritime patrol mission in late January 1941. The Condors reached the apex of their success in January–February 1941, when convoy defenses were still weak, but their period of dominance was short-lived. (Imperial War Museum HU 39426)

STRATEGIC SITUATION

The strategic situation turned drastically against Great Britain with the German occupation of Norway by June 8, 1940, and the capitulation of France on June 22. British pre-war planning by the Admiralty for trade protection had not expected the Luftwaffe to pose a significant threat in the Atlantic. Instead, the sudden German victories in Norway and France gave the predatory Luftwaffe and Kriegsmarine unprecedented access to Britain's transatlantic trade routes. Operating from French bases, even medium-range German aircraft could now attack British shipping in the Southwest Approaches, the Irish Sea and on the convoy routes to Gibraltar. Just as enemy attack against convoys stepped up in August 1940, the Royal Navy was forced to keep a significant portion of its strength – including destroyers – in home waters to deter a possible German invasion.

Hitler's main strategic objective after the fall of France was to force Britain to the negotiating table in order to gain an armistice, so that Germany could then throw its full weight against the Soviet Union. Never sanguine about conducting an amphibious invasion across the English Channel (despite the overt preparations for Operation *Seelöwe*), Hitler preferred to exert pressure on Britain's sea lines of communications to bring about the country's submission. He was receptive to both Großadmiral Erich Raeder's recommendations to step up the war against Britain's merchant convoys with his U-boats and surface raiders, and to Reichsmarschall Hermann Göring's claims that his Luftwaffe could smash the RAF and then close Britain's ports by bombing and mining them. This strategy appeared to offer the Third Reich a low-cost way to drive Britain out of the war, without risking a potential bloodbath in the English Channel. Accordingly, Hitler declared a total blockade of the British Isles on August 17, 1940,

An Fw 200 C-3/U-4 in Greece in late 1941. This aircraft was sent to the Mediterranean to mount a special attack on British shipping in the Suez Canal but was shot down over Port Said on September 5, 1941. The diversion of scarce aircraft to secondary missions seriously impaired KG 40's operations against British convoys. (HITM Archives 77991)

and authorized the Kriegsmarine and Luftwaffe to sever Britain's economic lifelines. Consequently, the role of the Fw 200 Condor anti-shipping operations should be considered in the context of the German strategic dynamic in 1940–41, which consisted of five concurrent but uncoordinated campaigns: air raids on ports, mining of coastal ports, and air, U-boat and surface warship attacks on convoys. If these campaigns were properly coordinated, Germany had the means to strangle the British war economy. Yet the OKW failed to efficiently synchronize these five campaigns against British shipping and allowed the Luftwaffe and Kriegsmarine to conduct independent operations.

Generalfeldmarschall Hugo Sperrle's *Luftflotte* 3 began attacks against British convoys in the Irish Sea with He 111 and Ju 88 bombers, but these aircraft only had an effective anti-shipping radius of operations of about 805km (500 miles). Given this range restriction, the medium bombers had little time to search for maritime targets at sea and had to operate within range of British land-based fighters. The Fw 200 C, with an effective range that was triple that of other bombers, was the only aircraft that could conduct maritime air reconnaissance and anti-shipping operations beyond the range of British land-based fighters. Among the new tenants moving into French air bases soon after the 1940 armistice was a detachment of KG 40. It first operated from Brest in July, but then on August 2, 1940, began deploying to Bordeaux-Merignac, the same airbase from which Charles de Gaulle had fled on June 17. By mid-August, Major Petersen had nine Fw 200s on hand, but operational readiness for the early C-1 model Condors rarely exceeded 30 percent. The first batch of Fw 200 C-1s had been rushed into service and after just moderate use in the Norwegian Campaign, many were sidelined by cracks in their fuselage and faulty brakes. Although the RLM placed orders for more and improved Fw 200s after the fall of France, Focke-Wulf was only able to deliver another 20 aircraft to I/KG 40 in the last six months of 1940. Amazingly, Focke-Wulf continued deliveries of civilian Fw 200 models to Lufthansa.

Initially, the Luftwaffe did not know how to use the Fw 200 to best advantage. In July 1940, I/KG 40 fell under the 9. *Flieger-Division* of Sperrle's *Luftflotte* 3, which decided to employ the Condors in the aerial minelaying campaign. I/KG 40 conducted 12 night minelaying missions in British and Irish waters between July 15 and 27, which resulted in the loss of two Condors. Petersen complained about this costly misuse of his aircraft and at the end of July, I/KG 40 was switched back to maritime reconnaissance. Nevertheless, Petersen continued to argue for using the Fw 200s in an anti-shipping role and after Hitler's blockade order, Sperrle decided to unleash Petersen's Condors against the relatively unprotected British shipping west of Ireland. Even though Petersen rarely had more than four operational aircraft in 1940, his group began to steadily sink and damage enemy freighters around Ireland, and it was soon clear that the Condor had found its niche in the war.

When the Condor attacks began, Great Britain had four main convoy routes that were vulnerable to long-range air strikes: the HX and SC convoys on the Halifax-to-Liverpool run; the OA and OB convoys on the route between the southern British ports and Halifax; the HG and OG convoys running between Gibraltar and Liverpool; and the SL convoys from Sierra Leone to Liverpool. A snapshot of shipping on August 17, 1940, for example, would have shown 13 convoys at sea on these routes, made up of 531 merchant vessels and 22 escort warships. Most convoys received a strong escort three days out from Liverpool, but they crossed the Atlantic with minimal protection. The greatest danger of Condor attack therefore occurred when poorly escorted convoys were still about 965km (600 miles) out from Liverpool or Gibraltar and were beyond the range of effective land-based air cover.

Despite the Condor's early successes against weakly defended British shipping, the Luftwaffe failed miserably to use KG 40 to best advantage in supporting U-boat attacks on convoys. With a limited number of operational aircraft available, KG 40 could

Condors at their most vulnerable – on the ground. An RAF aerial reconnaissance photo taken of Værnes airfield in Normway in July 1942 reveals ten Fw 200s on the runway. The RAF had very good intelligence on KG 40's activities but air raids on Værnes only damaged two Condors. Note that the Condors are not protected by revetements or other anti-blast barriers. (Author's collection)

only shadow a convoy for three to four hours and lacked sufficient aircraft to maintain contact for an extended period. In essence, KG 40 was only capable of sporadic maritime reconnaissance, not the consistent surveillance that the U-boats needed. Both Raeder and his U-boat chief, Vizeadmiral Karl Dönitz, were incensed that their small number of U-boats at sea had to waste valuable time searching for British convoys while the Luftwaffe failed to provide adequate maritime reconnaissance. Prior to the war, Raeder had lost the argument with Göring about creating an independent naval air arm to support the fleet and now the Luftwaffe High Command was unwilling to commit major resources to support maritime operations.

On the other side of the Channel, the Admiralty initially responded to the Condor threat with a variety of *ad hoc* measures. As a quick fix, the 5,000-ton freighter HMS *Crispin* was converted into a disguised anti-aircraft vessel, armed with a 100mm (4in) high-angle AA gun and six of the new 20mm Oerlikon guns. *Crispin* would pretend to be a merchant vessel trailing behind a convoy, in the hope of attracting a low-level attack. However, after several months of dull escort duty without sighting a Condor, it was sunk by a U-boat on February 3, 1941. Given that the Q-ship had to follow alone behind the convoy in order to attract air attacks, it lacked survivability in U-boat patrolled waters and the Admiralty decided not to sacrifice any more crews in this role.

Churchill pressed the Admiralty to improve convoy anti-air defenses as rapidly as possible, but these emergency measures would take months to implement. In the interim, Churchill suggested a Commando raid against KG 40's airbase at Bordeaux using a single Danish-owned civilian Fw 200 in a "Trojan horse" operation. The plan called for the aircraft, repainted in Luftwaffe colors, to land at Bordeaux at night. The two dozen troops on board would then disembark and destroy every Condor on the base. Although such a raid might have severely disrupted KG 40's operations for a while, there was no viable extraction plan for the raiding force, so the Commandos sensibly backed off from an obvious suicide mission.

In November 1940, Britain's only real offensive tool was RAF Bomber Command and Churchill redirected it squarely at the Fw 200 threat by ordering raids against Bordeaux-Merignac airfield and the Focke-Wulf plant in Bremen. The first raid on Bordeaux-Merignac took place on the night of November 22–23, 1940, and saw 32 bombers destroy four hangars and two Fw 200s on the ground. Three follow-up raids were unsuccessful and it was not until the raid on April 13, 1941, that three more Condors were destroyed at the base. Bomber Command continued to raid the airfield on occasion, but Luftwaffe anti-aircraft defenses improved to the point that no more Condors were destroyed on the ground. Given that Bomber Command's aircraft had little ability to hit point targets at night and were generally missing their aim points by about 3km (2 miles) or more in 1940–41, the fact that 191 sorties on Bordeaux-Merignac destroyed five Condors on the ground is remarkable. The first major raid against the Focke-Wulf plant did not occur until January 1, 1941, and although it caused some minor disruption in Condor production, it only encouraged the company to shift much of the Fw 200 production inland to Cottbus.

Despite the inability of the British to intercept Fw 200s over water or destroy their bases and factories, the duel between the Condors and the British Atlantic convoys was

ultimately shaped by each side's different approach to inter-service cooperation. In order to make Hitler's blockade work, the Luftwaffe and the Kriegsmarine had to work together, which included using the Fw 200s to support anti-convoy operations in conjunction with the ongoing U-boat campaign. However, both services constantly squabbled over the best way to use KG 40's Condors. Göring was more concerned about maintaining control over his air units than in helping the U-boats deliver a knockout blow against Britain's convoys. Raeder temporarily gained Kriegsmarine control over KG 40 (while Göring was on Christmas holiday) when he sent Dönitz to brief the OKW on how the Condors could support the U-boat campaign. Dönitz claimed: "Just let me have a minimum of 20 Fw 200s solely for reconnaissance purposes and the U-boat successes will shoot up!" Hitler obliged Dönitz by ordering I/KG 40 to be subordinated to the Kriegsmarine on January 6, 1941, but as soon as Göring returned from holiday he pressed Hitler to reverse his decision. Two months later, Hitler gave in and returned I/KG 40 to Luftwaffe control, but authorized the creation of the *Fliegerführer Atlantik* in Lorient to better synchronize Luftwaffe support for maritime operations. Generalmajor Martin Harlinghausen from IX.*Fliegerkorps* was appointed to this post and he made every effort to increase cooperation between KG 40 and the U-boats. Nevertheless, the Luftwaffe continued to divert KG 40's planes and aircrew away from maritime operations to support special projects.

On the other hand, the Admiralty and the RAF were quick to realize that there was no single-service solution to the Condor attacks and they were able to harmonize their inter-service operations far better than the Germans. Although initially preoccupied by the Battle of Britain, the RAF eventually began to commit more and better aircraft to Coastal Command, enabling it to contest Condor operations by 1942. The RAF was also quick to supply pilots and Hurricanes for the CAM ships, even at a time when it was still hard-pressed in the skies over southern England. From the British viewpoint, the duel between its Atlantic convoys and the Condors represented a "catch-up" dynamic, with both the RAF and Royal Navy struggling to redress their pre-war mistakes in the field of trade protection. Like the Germans, the British had the means at hand to defeat the poorly coordinated enemy anti-shipping operations, but they had to do so quickly before irreparable harm was done to Britain's wartime economy.

A photograph of convoy OG 75 taken from a Condor in early October 1941. Although KG 40 was able to shadow the Gibraltar-bound convoy on and off for eight days, the U-boats failed to sink a single merchant ship. Note that from this low-level angle, the convoy is clearly skylined against the horizon. (Author's collection)

29

TECHNICAL SPECIFICATIONS

THE Fw 200'S COMBAT CAPABILITIES

The Condor's combat prowess rested on three primary capabilities: its ability to find targets, to hit targets and then to evade enemy defenses. In 1940 the Condor had only a rudimentary capability of finding convoys and other suitable merchant targets. On a typical mission, an Fw 200 would fly about 1,500km from Bordeaux to look for targets west of Ireland, which would give the aircraft about three hours to conduct its search. Normally, Condors flew quite low (about 500–600m off the water), which made it easier to spot ships outlined against the horizon and avoided giving the enemy too much early warning. From this low altitude, the Condor could search an area of approximately 320x120km (200x75 miles), with several of its crew scanning the horizon with binoculars. In decent weather, which was rare in the Atlantic, the observers might be able to spot a convoy up to 15–20km (10–12 miles) away, but cloud cover could reduce this by half. In 1941, improved Condors with longer range had four hours on-station time, increasing the search area by about 25 percent. When the Condors gained a search-radar capability with the FuG 200 Hohentwiel radar in December 1942 and their on-station endurance doubled, their search area increased to nearly four times the size it had been in 1940. The Hohentwiel radar could detect surface targets up to 80km (50 miles) distant and its beam was 41km (25 miles) wide at that range. Nevertheless, the perennial problem remained for the Condors that due to limited numbers, KG 40 had difficulty maintaining a consistent presence along known convoy routes. With one sortie sent every day or so for three to eight hours, there was no guarantee that they would be operational at the very time a convoy was

Fw 200 CONDOR C-3 COCKPIT

1. Undercarriage de-icing cock
2. Suction-air throw-over switch (starboard)
3. Suction-air throw-over switch (port)
4. Instrument panel lighting switch (port)
5. Pilot's oxygen pressure gauge
6. NACA cowling floodlight switch
7. Pilot's control column
8. Intercom switch
9. Clock
10. Illumination buttons
11. Pilot's repeater compass
12. Airspeed indicator
13. Gyro-compass course indicator
14. Turn-and-bank indicator
15. Coarse-fine altimeter
16. External temperature gauge
17. Rate-of-climb indicator
18. Artificial horizon
19. Coarse altimeter
20. Fuselage flap control lamp
21. Fuselage flap release handle
22. Radio beacon visual indicator
23. Gyro-compass
24. Gyro-compass heating indicator
25. Gyro-compass heating switch
26. Pilot's rudder pedal
27. Pilot's rudder pedal
28. Pilot's seat pan (seat-back removed for clarity)
29. Compass installation
30. RPM indicator (port outer)

31. RPM indicator (port inner)
32. RPM indicator (starboard inner)
33. RPM indicator (starboard outer)
34. Double manifold pressure gauges (port engines)
35. Oil and fuel pressure gauges (port engines)
36. Oil and fuel pressure gauges (starboard engines)
37. Double manifold pressure gauges (starboard engines)
38. Pitch indicator (port outer)
39. Emergency bomb release
40. Pitch indicator (port inner)
41. Bomb-arming lever
42. Pitch indicator (starboard inner)
43. Pitch indicator (starboard outer)
44. Oil temperature gauge (port outer)
45. Oil temperature gauge (port inner)
46. Oil temperature gauge (starboard inner)
47. Oil temperature gauge (starboard outer)
48. Instrument panel dimmer switch
49. Undercarriage and landing flap indicators
50. Starter selector switch
51. Master battery cut-off switch
52. Ignition switches (port)
53. Ignition switches (starboard)
54. Landing light switch
55. Servo unit emergency button

56. UV-lighting switch
57. Longitudinal trim emergency switch
58. Directional trim emergency switch
59. Longitudinal trim indicator
60. Throttles
61. Supercharger levers
62. Fuel tank selectors
63. Throttle locks
64. Directional trim indicator
65. Directional trim switch
66. Undercarriage retraction lever
67. Airscrew pitch control levers (port)
68. Airscrew pitch control levers (starboard)
69. Wing flap lever
70. Parking switch activating handle
71. Fuel safety cock levers (port tanks)
72. Servo unit emergency pull-out knob
73. Fire extinguisher pressure gauge
74. Fuel safety cock levers (starboard tanks)
75. Fire extinguishers (port engines)
76. Fire extinguishers (starboard engines)
77. RPM synchronization selector switch
78. Remote compass course indicator
79. Pitot head heating indicator
80. Airspeed indicator
81. Turn-and-bank indicator

82. Rate-of-climb indicator
83. Control surface temperature gauge
84. Coarse-fine altimeter
85. Artificial horizon
86. Cylinder temperature gauge
87. Cylinder temperature throw-over switch
88. Starting fuel contents gauge
89. Cruise fuel contents gauge
90. Cruise fuel transfer switch
91. Clock
92. Starting fuel transfer switch
93. Oil contents gauge
94. Starter switches
95. Suction and pressure gauges for undercarriage de-icing and gyro devices
96. Injection valve press buttons
97. Hydraulic systems pressure gauge
98. Windcreen heating
99. Control surfaces temperature switch
100. Fuel pump switches (port tanks)
101. Fuel pump switches (starboard tanks)
102. Controllable-gill adjustment
103. Airscrew de-icing levers (starboard engines)
104. Co-pilot's seat pan (seat-back removed for clarity)
105. Co-pilot's rudder pedal
106. Co-pilot's rudder pedal
107. Co-pilot's control column

passing through the area. Thus the Condor's actual ability to find targets was rather sporadic until late in the war, which accounts for the fact that KG 40 missed more convoys than it found.

As a converted civilian aircraft, the Fw 200's ability to hit targets was severely limited by the lack of a proper bombsight and poor forward visibility. From the beginning, it was obvious that the Fw 200 could not attack in the way a normal bomber did, but had to rely on low-level attack (*Tiefangriff*) tactics. Approaching as low as 45m off the water at 290km/h (180mph), a Condor would release one or two bombs at a distance of about 240m (790ft) from the target. This method ensured a high probability that the bomb would either strike the ship directly or detonate in the water alongside, causing damage. Although the early Condors only carried a load of four 250kg bombs, the low-level method made it highly likely that at least one ship would be sunk or damaged on each sortie that found a target. Since most civilian freighters were unarmored and lacked robust damage control, even moderate damage inflicted would often prove fatal. KG 40 became so adept at low-level tactics in early 1941 that some attacks scored three out of four hits. However, many of the bombs that struck the target failed to explode due to improper fusing – a nagging problem for the low-level method. Once the Condors shifted to attacks from 3,000m (9,840ft) with the Lotfe 7D bombsight, which had a circular error probability of 91m (300ft) with a single bomb against a stationary target, about one bomb in three landed close enough to inflict at least some damage. The Condors were also capable of low-level machine gun strafing. In 1940, a Condor using the low-level attack profile only had time to fire a single 75-round drum of ball ammunition from the MG 15 machine gun in the gondola during each eight-second pass on a ship. This type of strafing inflicted little damage. Oberleutnant Bernhard Jope made three strafing runs on the *Empress of Britain* and wounded only one person on the vessel. When improved Condors mounted larger 13mm and 20mm weapons in the gondola, firing AP-T and HEI-T ammunition, their strafing became far deadlier and the superstructures of merchant ships proved highly vulnerable to this type of fire. However, once Allied defenses made low-level attacks too costly, the strafing capability of Condors was effectively neutralized.

The Condor's ability to maneuver, absorb damage, and evade enemy interception was always problematic. The Fw 200 B was built to fly in thin air at medium altitudes, with no sharp maneuvering. Tank made the aircraft's remarkable long range possible by designing a very lightweight airframe. Early military versions lacked armor plate, self-sealing fuel tanks or structural strengthening and the Condor was at least 2–4 tons lighter than other four-engined bombers in this class. Unlike purpose-built bombers that had some armor plate and redundant flight controls, the Condor was always exceedingly vulnerable to damage. When moderately damaged by a hit, chunks of the fuselage or tail often fell off, and the underpowered aircraft had difficulty staying in the air if it lost one of its engines. Even worse, there were six large unarmored fuel tanks inside the cabin, which could turn the Condor into a blazing torch if hit by tracer ammunition. When Condors tried to maneuver sharply to avoid enemy flak or fighters, their weak structure could be damaged, leading to metal fatigue, cracks and loss of the aircraft. Defensive armament was initially weak but had improved greatly by the C-4 variant, causing enemy fighters to avoid lengthy gun duels with Fw 200s. Since the Condors were usually operating close to the water, they did not normally have to worry about fighter attacks from below, but this also severely limited their options. At these low altitudes, they were unable to dive and they could not out-turn or outrun an opponent. This limited them to "jinking" to upset an opponent's aim, hoping that the A- and B-stand gunners would score a lucky hit on the pursuing fighter. Thus the Condor essentially had poor evasion capabilities, which ultimately was a major contributor to its operational failure.

ARMED VARIANTS OF THE Fw 200 CONDOR

Focke-Wulf built the Fw 200 at its Bremen plant and later expanded to Cottbus once RAF bombing began to interfere with production. The Fw 200 remained in production until February 1944 but was never accorded a very high priority by the RLM since it was essentially supporting a Kriegsmarine mission. Furthermore, in 1939 Focke-Wulf only had two aircraft types in low-rate production for the Luftwaffe – the Fw 189 and the Fw 200 – but by 1941 the company was shifting to mass production of the Fw 190 fighter. By 1942, Condor production was little more than a legacy program, while Kurt Tank focused his main design talent on developing improved fighters.

Year	Fw 200s Built	Fw 200s Lost (All causes)
1940	42	14
1941	52	35
1942	96	32
1943	77	52

Fw 200 C-0 and C-1

The first production batch saw ten aircraft built between December 1939 and May 1940. The aircraft were not originally equipped with the ventral gondola and were primarily reconnaissance versions, but all were rebuilt as C-1 bombers in the summer of 1940. The Fw 200 C-1 had a five-man crew, four 830hp BMW 132H-1 engines, and was armed with five 7.92mm MG 15 machine guns.

Fw 200 C-2

Eight of this model were built through July and August 1940. They incorporated minor improvements based upon lessons learned in the Norwegian Campaign.

An Fw 200 C-8 at Bordeaux in August 1943, has Hohentwiel radar aerials mounted on its nose and a Lotfe 7D bombsight mounted at the front of the gondola. This was the final version of the Condor and it enjoyed a brief period of success in mid-1943. (HITM Archives 77992)

Fw 200 C-3

Focke-Wulf began to build the significantly improved Fw 200 C-3 version in September 1940, which was the first model really designed for combat. In addition to strengthening the fuselage to bear a heavy bomb and fuel load, modest armor plating and self-sealing fuel tanks were added. Kurt Tank also upgraded the powerplant to four 1,000hp Bramo 323 R-2 radial engines. The crew was increased to seven. Nine different defensive variations were introduced, with armament in the four defensive positions ranging from 7.92mm MG 15s to 13mm MG 131s. An offensive weapon station was created at the front of the gondola for a 20mm MG 151 cannon, which was used for strafing ships. The C-3 could theoretically carry up to 2,900kg of bombs but normally carried the standard four 250kg bombs with extra external fuel tanks instead, which increased the strike radius to 1,750km (1,090 miles). A total of 52 Fw 200 C-3s were built by March 1942.

Fw 200 C-4

Between March 1942 and May 1943 a total of 107 of the C-4 models were built. Focke-Wulf re-equipped the A-stand with a powered FW 19 turret with a 20mm MG 151/20 cannon and the B- and C-stands were upgraded to 13mm MG 131 heavy machine guns. The crude Revi sight was replaced with the much-improved Lotfe 7D bombsight. The Condor also gained surface search radar: the early C-4s carried an FuG Atlas or Rostock set while later variants were given the FuG 200 Hohentwiel radar. These modifications added more than one ton to the aircraft's weight, which made it 30km/h (19mph) slower than its predecessor.

Fw 200 C-5 and C-6

A total of 22 Fw 200 C-5s were built between March and September 1943, while only 16 C-6s were built between June 1942 and June 1943. Both models represented only incremental improvements over the C-4 model and their increased weight further degraded performance. Some of the C-6 models were modified to carry Hs-293 guided bombs in late 1943.

Fw 200 C-8

The final version of the Fw 200 entered production in August 1943 and only nine were built when all Condor production ceased in February 1944. Another 17 older models were also converted to C-8 standard. The C-8 was designed for stand-off attacks and was outfitted with FuG 203b Kehl III missile-control equipment for up to two Hs-293 guided bombs.

CONVOY DEFENSE CAPABILITIES

In the duel against the Condors, the two critical convoy defensive capabilities were the ability to detect and to hit aerial intruders. Initially, convoys were almost totally dependent upon the "Mark I eyeball" to spot Condors. In the Atlantic, where visual detection ranges were often just 10km (6 miles) or less, an attacking Condor at 50m height approaching at 290km/h (180mph) could be on top of a target in just two minutes, leaving very little reaction time. Air guards were few in early convoys and ships travelling alone were often unaware they were under attack until the bombs began to fall. Nor did convoys receive any early warning from external sources, such as ULTRA or other signals intelligence (SIGINT). Being virtually blind to the

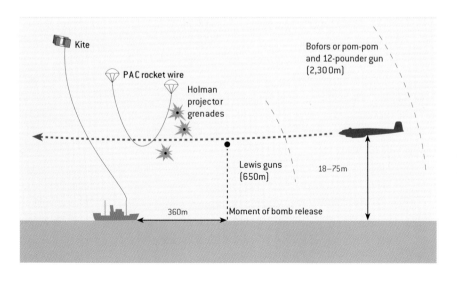

From a German diagram showing the variety of Allied responses to low-level attack, ranging from AA guns to rocket-launched cables. Note that this diagram shows a bows-on attack, when most attacks occurred either from astern or abeam.

A pre-war photo of the passenger liner SS *Empress of Britain*, set on fire by Fw 200 attack on October 26, 1940. Since the vessel was provided with a 6in gun, a 12-pounder AA gun and six Lewis Guns, the Admiralty believed that she was adequately armed to sail independently, but she also proved to be too big a target to miss from a height of only 50m. (Author's collection)

approaching intruder significantly added to their vulnerability to Condor attack in 1940–41. The situation began to improve with the introduction of Type 281 air surveillance radar in February 1941, although few were available to convoys until 1942. When available, a Type 281 radar could detect a Condor up to 110km (70 miles) out from the convoy. This would provide some early warning and allow the convoy commodore to track the intruder and alter course as soon as the aircraft left for home. By 1942, British Intelligence also began to help, with the RAF's Y-Service sometimes successful in detecting Fw 200 radio transmissions over the Bay of Biscay. Later that year, even Flower class corvettes were being equipped with short-range air surveillance radar and convoys gained an excellent situational awareness of approaching Condors, which then enabled them to coordinate with the RAF for air cover as necessary.

Once a Condor was spotted, the convoy's ability to hit the intruder varied from negligible in 1940 to quite robust in 1943. Pre-war estimates confidently calculated that a quad .50cal Mk III mount on a destroyer firing 500 rounds in a ten-second burst would achieve 40 hits against a bomber-sized target. In reality, it usually took thousands of rounds to hit a fast-moving target from the deck of a ship that was pitching up and down and from side to side. Even though a number of DEMS ships were equipped with the 12-pdr (76.2mm) HA anti-aircraft gun, which could theoretically engage a Condor out to 6–8km (4–5 miles), the Admiralty only authorized merchant crews to engage unidentified aircraft within 800m (2,600ft) in order to reduce friendly-fire incidents. This was not unreasonable since DEMS ships often fired on RAF aircraft as well, but it effectively reduced the defensive umbrella to point-blank range and prevented convoys from establishing anything like an area defense. Furthermore, the elderly 12-pdr firing AA rounds was not optimized for medium altitudes, nor was the quad 2-pdr (40mm) "pom-pom" best at dealing with low-altitude attacks. Instead, convoys were heavily dependent upon short-range fire from elderly Marlin (7.62mm), Hotchkiss (8mm), and Lewis (7.9mm) machine guns, which fired low-velocity ball ammunition and were prone to jamming. Typically, a merchant ship would only get a chance to fire one or two 47-round drums from a Lewis gun as the Condor sped away, perhaps damaging the tail or rear fuselage. At Churchill's urging, the Admiralty also developed a variety of *ad hoc* anti-air weapons such as the Holman projector, the Parachute Aerial Cable (PAC), the Fast Aerial Mine (FAM) and even 3in rockets, which were installed on some merchant ships in late 1940 and early 1941. These makeshift weapons were all dismal failures and never claimed a Condor or seriously interfered with KG 40's anti-shipping attacks. However, it was the widespread installation of 20mm Oerlikons on convoys in 1942 that provided effective defense against low-level strikes. The Oerlikon had the range and muzzle velocity to engage Condors out to 2,000m and its API-T ammunition was perfect for setting the Fw 200's vulnerable fuel tanks ablaze. The Condors regained some immunity with mid-level attacks in 1943 but this was soon redressed by the 40mm Bofors gun, which could engage aircraft up to 3,000m. By late 1943, convoy air defenses were strong enough to deter or defeat all but the most determined Condor attacks.

The Admiralty also sought to provide some passive defenses for merchant ships to protect them from Condor strafing attacks. Since most armor plate was earmarked for warship construction, another *ad hoc* solution was found in developing lightweight "plastic armor" for merchant ships, which consisted of screw-on panels made from a mix of bitumen and granite chippings. This "plastic armor" was applied on bridge superstructures and around AA guns on DEMS vessels, affording at least some protection from enemy machine gun fire.

However, it was not enough for convoys simply to deter Condor attack, for if the aircraft were allowed to remain in the vicinity, they could shadow the convoy and guide in U-boat wolfpacks. Until the arrival of CAM ships and escort carriers in mid-1941, convoys had no ability to intercept shadowing Condors. The CAM ships proved to be of limited use, because once a vessel's single Hurricane had been expended, they reverted to being just a normal merchant ship, while the Condors might operate against a single convoy for several days or more. On the other hand, the escort carrier could provide continuous daylight air cover over a convoy and the Martlet fighter proved very adept at intercepting the Fw 200. Before 1944, only a few convoys had an escort carrier sailing with them, but as cooperation with the RAF and USAAF improved, convoys by 1943 increasingly gained land-based air cover. In time, through a combination of embarked aviation and cooperation with shore-based aircraft, convoys gained an impressive ability to intercept aerial intruders.

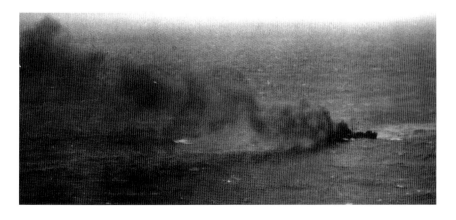

The 5,702-ton freighter SS *Starstone* on fire west of Ireland on October 31, 1940, after attack by an Fw 200 Condor. Like many merchantmen at this time, it was armed with just a couple of machine guns. However, *Starstone* did not sink and returned to service in early 1941. (Author's collection)

THE COMBATANTS

THE Fw 200 CREW

During the course of the war, the size of the Fw 200 crew increased from five members to six, and finally to seven. Each aircraft had a *flugzeugführer* (pilot) and co-pilot/bombardier, as well as a *bordfunker* (radio operator), *bordmechaniker* (aerial mechanic), and a *bordschütz* (aerial gunner). As defensive armament increased, another *bordschütz* was needed and in 1943, another *bordfunker* was added to operate the radar. The airmen on Condors required a great deal of training and experience to function as a well-knit team on this complicated multi-engined aircraft. Small mistakes, such as failing to properly monitor fuel flow to the engines in a shallow dive, would lead to aircraft losses. Also, the Fw 200 crews often had to operate alone, almost always over water and at great distances from any friendly assistance. Crews had to learn to be efficient and self-reliant to avoid ending up at the bottom of the Atlantic.

In the beginning, KG 40 benefited from a cadre of Lufthansa aircrew with some experience on the Fw 200, although commercial passenger missions were considerably different from low-level anti-shipping attacks. Even experienced pilots like Edgar Petersen had to learn through experience the difficult art of finding convoys at sea. In August 1940, with only a handful of aircrew having any experience in low-level anti-shipping strikes, KG 40 had to gradually familiarize its personnel with their unique mission, and develop a set of effective tactical procedures as the best means to attack enemy shipping. Petersen was sparing of his crews and precious aircraft and he wisely refused to commit crews to long-range Atlantic missions until he judged they were ready, which limited the group to a low sortie rate in the fall of

MAJOR EDGAR PETERSEN

Edgar Petersen (1904–86) earned his commercial pilot's license in the 1920s. Although ostensibly a civilian pilot, Petersen took part in a secret program to train military pilots and he was sent to conduct clandestine military flight training in the Soviet Union in 1929. When the Luftwaffe was created in 1935, Petersen was already a veteran civil pilot and he was brought in to become director of the Instrument Flying School at Celle. Around 1937, Petersen became a member of Oberstleutnant Theodor Rowehl's special long-range reconnaissance unit and participated in covert missions around Great Britain and in the Baltic. In the years before radar was operational, Rowehl successfully used civilian airliners and pilots working for the Luftwaffe to penetrate foreign airspace and photograph naval bases and other potential targets. In 1938, Petersen went back to teaching a course on long-distance navigation over water to Luftwaffe pilots and as war approached, Hauptmann Petersen was attached to X.*Fliegerkorps* as a maritime reconnaissance specialist. With this background, Petersen was a natural choice to lead the first Fw 200 Condor unit when it was formed in October 1939.

(Bundesarchiv, Bild 183-B19957)

Petersen served as the first commander of I/KG 40 from November 1939 to April 1941, then became KG 40's *Geschwaderkommodore* until August 1941. Although primarily a reconnaissance pilot, he was quick to realize the potential of armed Condors and he was the driving force that rapidly built up KG 40 from scratch to a formidable combat team in just a year. Petersen was skillful at gathering resources and pilots for the new *gruppe* from a Luftwaffe High Command that was ambivalent about what a handful of converted airliners could accomplish. Indeed, Petersen had to spend a great deal of effort fending off attempts to divert his Fw 200s onto other missions such as minelaying or bombing port facilities. He was constantly frustrated by the low priority assigned to the Fw 200 Condor, which made it difficult for him to build up a sizeable strike force and he even made a direct appeal to Hitler to place more emphasis on the anti-shipping mission.

In addition to his administrative duties, Petersen was also an excellent combat leader and he personally led some of KG 40's earliest long-range missions over the Atlantic. He was responsible for several of the early sinkings off western Ireland in October 1940, for which he was awarded KG 40's first *Ritterkreuz*. Promoted to major, Petersen spent much of 1941 organizing the second *gruppe* of KG 40 and working to ensure closer cooperation with the Kriegsmarine's U-boat campaign. It was Petersen who made the first multi-Condor attacks on convoys in early 1941, exploiting the weakness of British air defenses. It is fair to say that it was Edgar Petersen who turned the Fw 200 into the "scourge of the Atlantic" that worried Churchill so much.

In August 1941 Petersen was ordered to take six Condors from I/KG 40 and proceed to Greece as *Suez-Kommando* in order to conduct attacks against British shipping in the Suez Canal. These attacks were failures and Petersen was soon sent back to Berlin to join the OKL's Trials and Research Unit (*Versuchtverband Oberkommando der Luftwaffe*) to participate in the He 177 bomber's flight trials. Petersen was eventually promoted to Oberst and given command of the trials unit, in which he remained until the end of the war. During 1942–45 he was involved in the flight-testing of a number of late-model aircraft, including the Do 335 *Pfeil* fighter. Petersen survived the war and died in 1986.

Oberleutnant Heinrich Schlosser (1908–90) served with KG 40 from May 1940 until July 1942. Off Norway, Schlosser was responsible for the first ship sunk by a Condor, and went on to become one of KG 40's top pilots. He was awarded the *Ritterkreuz* in December 1941. Afterwards, Schlosser was involved in evaluating the He 177 bomber and served in training units, which enabled him to survive the war. He later made *Oberst* in the post-war *Bundeswehr*. (Bundesarchiv, Bild 183-2008-1118-500)

1940. Under these circumstances, I/KG 40 was not a fully trained or combat-ready group until spring 1941.

Like all Luftwaffe bomber pilots, the men who flew Fw 200s required about two years of flight training before they reached KG 40. After completing their initial flight training in the first year, they progressed to multi-engined aircraft, blind-flying school and advanced navigation. Once they had gone through the standard Luftwaffe pilot schooling, they were transferred to KG 40's conversion unit, IV(Erg)/KG 40, which was stationed in Germany until January 1942. This unit trained pilots and other aircrew on over-water operations using half-a-dozen of the original unarmed Fw 200s and some He 111s and Do 217s. In 1942, Condor conversion training was shifted to central France. The following year, the conversion group also began to conduct He 177 training, as the Fw 200 began to be replaced.

In 1940, all Condor pilots were officers, usually an *oberleutnant*, with the rest of the crew consisting of *feldwebels* or *unteroffiziers*, apart from the gunners, who were *obergefreiter*. By 1942, KG 40 was finding it difficult to keep up with high officer losses so more aircraft were flown by NCOs. During 1940–41, when KG 40's losses were few and the Nazi propaganda machine was quick to promote their successes, the morale of crews was high. Furthermore, when not flying, Bordeaux was a far more comfortable billet for the *kampfflieger* than that experienced by their comrades on the Eastern Front or in North Africa. However, once I/KG 40 began to suffer heavy combat losses and the vulnerability of their jury-rigged bombers became apparent, morale plummeted and those who could – including the surviving *Ritterkreuz* recipients – transferred to other units. By 1943, the crews in KG 40 were less well trained than their predecessors and more uncertain about their prospects on each mission.

A Condor pilot (left) and co-pilot on long-range patrol over the Atlantic. Despite the heavy flight gear and life-jackets, crews knew that in event of water landing they were beyond range of German air–sea rescue and their only hope might be rescue by the ships they had just attacked. (Author's collection)

THE ALLIES

The men on the Allied side who fought the Condors were a heterogeneous mix of Royal Navy, Royal Canadian Navy and USN sailors, RAF and FAA pilots, British Merchant Navy sailors, Army DEMS gunners, RCN and US Army Air Force pilots. The merchant sailors, aided by Royal Navy and British Army gunners, were the only ones to carry the fight against the Condors for the entire period of 1940–44 and they were to suffer the most casualties from Condor attacks. Although latecomers to the duel, American pilots began to play a significant role in defeating the Condors by 1943.

The RAF pilots who manned the Hurricanes on CAM ships were some of the boldest of the Condors' opponents, but they had few chances to test their skills. Usually they were given one or two "trial" launches from land-based catapults before deployment. Unlike carrier pilots, however, they got no flight time during a convoy mission except in the rare case of a Condor sighting, and would have to spend up to two weeks on a merchantmen, enduring tedium and bad weather. Each CAM ship carried three pilots, which enabled them to take turns in two-hour shifts during daylight, sitting in the cockpit of the Hurricane atop the catapult. The CAM pilot could not be certain that, after weeks of exposure to salt water, his Hurricane would function properly, or that he would survive the obligatory post-mission ditching. Initially, the RAF only expected about half the CAM pilots to survive their one mission, although fortunately this proved to be overly pessimistic. In between deployments, CAM pilots were given an opportunity to gain flight hours before they went to sea again, to endure more long days awaiting the possibility of a single, brief mission.

In contrast, the FAA pilots who served on HMS *Audacity* and the later escort carriers usually gained a great deal of flying experience since the escort commanders wanted them up from dawn to dusk. Typically the fighter group was divided into sections of two Martlet fighters each, which could conduct a two-hour patrol over their convoy, looking for U-boats or Condors. Many pilots were able to attack surfaced U-boats, which kept them more actively engaged in the convoy's defense than the

Merchant sailors being taught aircraft identification and anti-aircraft gunnery principles using models. Early in the war, DEMS gunners tended to fire on any aircraft that approached a convoy, including RAF Coastal Command escorts. (Imperial War Museum A 5249)

Army maritime gunners cleaning an Oerlikon gun aboard a merchant ship. Defeating the Condors involved a truly joint-service effort on Britain's part, including contributions by all three services. By comparison, cooperation between the Kriegsmarine and Luftwaffe was poor and undermined Germany ability to defeat the convoys. (Imperial War Museum A 17334)

one-shot CAM pilots. However, losses from accidents were more likely than from combat since landing on the escort carriers' small flight decks in heavy seas took its toll on even the best pilots.

The young merchant sailors and Royal Navy ratings who volunteered for the DEMS program went to HMS *Glendower* in north Wales for several weeks of gunnery training. Afterwards they were assigned to a pool in Liverpool and then drafted to various ships as convoys departed. Normally, each merchant ship would receive between three and six Royal Navy gunners to man the 12-pdrs and the medium-caliber MG mount, while merchant crewmen would assist as ammunition handlers. On occasion, even the merchant sailors were used to operate light anti-aircraft guns, although these untrained men often proved to be of little value. One merchant sailor in a Gibraltar convoy who fired a 20mm Oerlikon at German aircraft noted that he had no problem firing the weapon, but he had no idea how to reload it. In waters where air attack was possible, the handful of DEMS gunners had to remain at their posts on shifts of four hours on and four hours off, from dawn to dusk. For them, the war at sea was tedious and extremely dangerous due to both air and U-boat attack. During the course of the war nearly 5,000 of the 24,000 Royal Navy DEMS gunners were killed – a loss rate of more than 20 percent.

Approximately 14,000 soldiers, mostly from the Maritime Royal Artillery Regiment, also went to sea as gunners on merchant ships and 1,222 were killed. As with the DEMS program, the MRA filled its ranks with volunteers from other units, one of whom was 21-year old Private William Henry Poundall[2]. After training on 40mm Bofors for two months at Musselburgh in Scotland, Poundall deployed as part of a gun crew on the 45,000-ton ocean liner RMS *Aquitania*. Although many volunteers were attracted by the idea of seeing other parts of the world, Poundall found that the gun crews were cooped up aboard ship for up to six weeks at a time and then shifted to another ship once the convoy reached its intended destination.

2   Ambervalley (People's War Comes to Amber Valley Project), "Maritime Royal Artillery Gunner" (Article A2800126), in BBC, *WW2 People's War*, London, BBC (2004).

SUB-LIEUTENANT ERIC "WINKLE" BROWN

Eric Brown (1919–) was born in Edinburgh, Scotland. The son of a World War I RFC pilot, he experienced his first flight at the age of eight when his father took him up in an RAF biplane. He went with his father to the 1936 Olympic Games in Berlin when he was 17 and through his father's aviation connections there, Brown was introduced to Ernst Udet and Hanna Reitsch. Udet was impressed with the young Scotsman and invited him for an aerobatic demonstration in a trainer, which increased Brown's interest in aviation. Returning to Scotland, he entered Edinburgh University and joined the University Air Unit, where he received his initial flight instruction on Gloster Gauntlets. At university, Eric majored in German and in 1938, he was offered a scholarship by the Foreign Office to study in Germany. Once there, he renewed his acquaintance with Udet and Reitsch, from which he gained a great deal of insight into German aviation developments. He was still in Munich when war was declared in September 1939, and although arrested and interrogated by the SS, he was remarkably allowed to cross the border to Switzerland (his connections with Udet probably proving helpful).

(Author's collection)

Upon returning home, Brown was surprised to find that the RAF had no great demand for reserve pilots so he decided to switch to the Fleet Air Arm (FAA). Although he had already been through pilot training, Brown spent the period September 1939 to August 1940 being schooled in naval fighter training on Gloster Gladiators and Blackburn Skuas, which included simulated carrier deck landings but no actual experience with carriers. After nearly a year of unfocused training and just a whiff of combat, Brown was dispatched to join 802 Squadron, which was re-forming after the loss of the carrier HMS Glorious. This unit received ten American-built F4F Wildcat fighters (designated the "Martlet" in Royal Navy service) on November 23, 1940. Brown took some time to adjust to the new fighter, ditching one in a reservoir in the winter of 1940–41 and another in the Firth of Forth in front of a visiting Winston Churchill in May 1941. Brown and his squadron mates were assigned to the new auxiliary carrier HMS Audacity in July 1941, where they were each required to make six practice landings on its short deck before the vessel sailed on its first convoy escort. Brown served on HMS Audacity for less than five months but shot down two Fw 200s on the route to Gibraltar. Although some of his fellow pilots achieved success against the Condor with standard attacks from astern, Brown favored head-on attacks to kill the pilots, who were protected by very little armor. Miraculously, Brown survived the sinking of HMS Audacity in December 1941, but his days as a regular fighter pilot were over. In January 1942 he was posted to Farnborough and became a specialist at landing different types of aircraft on carriers or improvised carriers. Within a year and a half he had made 1,500 deck landings on 22 different vessels.

By late 1943, Brown gradually made the transition into the role of Royal Navy test pilot and became involved in evaluating captured enemy aircraft, including an He 177 bomber. Even before the final German surrender, he was armed with a broad authorization letter from Churchill and given command of a special test unit that was sent to Germany to seize and test the best German aircraft. Brown secured ten Arado 234 jet bombers for Farnborough and was able to fly both the Me-262 jet fighter and the Me-163 rocket fighter. While in Germany, Brown was permitted to interview the captured former Reichsmarschall Göring about German aviation programs.

Returning to England, Brown was directly involved in the British jet aircraft program and made naval history by landing a Sea Vampire jet on HMS Ocean on December 3, 1945 – the first jet landing on a carrier. In 1951, Lieutenant-Commander Brown was sent to the United States, where he was instrumental in convincing the US Navy to adopt steam catapults and angled flight-decks on its next generation aircraft carriers. In 1957, he was sent back to Germany to help the newly created Bundesmarine organize an independent naval air arm – a critical deficiency from World War II. In an amazing turn of events, while he was in Germany for a three-year tour, Focke-Wulf GMbH asked him to act as a part-time test pilot for the company. Afterwards, Brown was put in charge of weapons development for the Fleet Air Arm and served again in Germany as naval attaché in 1964–65. Brown retired from the Royal Navy with the rank of captain in 1970 and during the course of his 31-year career he set a world record of 2,407 carrier deck landings. He was also the most decorated pilot in the Fleet Air Arm and during one award ceremony, King George VI quipped, "not you again" when Brown approached him. Brown continued civilian flying until 1989 and he became a prolific aviation writer. At time of writing, aged 90, he was still active in aviation circles.

COMBAT

THE HAPPY TIME, AUGUST 1940–JUNE 1941

Condor operations from Bordeaux-Merignac began sporadically in mid-August 1940 and continued from that location until July 1943. The first operations were tentative and designated as armed reconnaissance sorties rather than as anti-shipping strikes. Three days after Hitler announced his blockade of the British Isles, the Condor's participation in events began inauspiciously when an Fw 200 C-1, sent to check for Allied shipping west of Ireland, developed mechanical difficulties and was forced to conduct a belly-landing near Mount Brandon on the southwest coast. Petersen was able to mount a few sorties with his remaining two operational Condors and they succeeded in sinking the SS *Goathland*, a 3,821-ton merchant ship sailing alone, on August 25. Five more ships were damaged west of Ireland by the end of August. Nor did the situation improve much in September, when the KG 40 sank just one Greek freighter and damaged nine other ships. A further small freighter was sunk on October 2 and the 20,000-ton troop transport *Oronsay* was damaged on October 8. At first, the British appeared somewhat oblivious to the threat. One British soldier aboard *Oronsay*, Jeffrey Jackson, noted the lack of response to the Condor attack: "I was so seasick that I didn't care what happened. Others must have felt the same, because not a shot was fired by anyone at the German bomber."

After eight weeks of limited operations, KG 40 had sunk only three ships totaling 11,000 tons and damaged 21 ships of about 90,000 tons. Bombing accuracy was poor, with most damage inflicted by near-misses. In reality the Condor appeared to have difficulty inflicting enough damage to actually sink ships and seemed to be more

of a nuisance than a lethal threat. Given that U-boats sank more than 500,000 tons of shipping in the same period, the British Admiralty was not unduly disturbed at the Fw 200's combat debut.

However, this attitude was forever altered when Oberleutnant Bernhard Jope took off from Bordeaux on the morning of October 26 on his first operational sortie and headed northwest toward Ireland. At 0920hrs, Jope's crew spotted a large ship sailing alone, about 112km (70 miles) northwest of the Irish coast. It was the 42,348-ton ocean liner *Empress of Britain*, returning to Glasgow after a troop-transport mission to Suez. Although *Empress of Britain* was armed with a 3in AA gun on its stern and six Lewis guns, its poorly trained gunners mistook the unfamiliar Condor for a friendly aircraft and did not open fire. Jope came in very low, attacking from the port beam, and dropped two bombs, one of which hit the aft superstructure. Jope's ventral gunner also strafed the ship with his MG 15. As the ship began to burn, the captain increased speed to 24 knots and ordered his gun crews to fire. Returning for a second pass, Jope had a harder time with a fast-moving target that was now firing at him and this time he failed to hit. Although one of his own engines had suffered damage from a Lewis gunner, in his final pass Jope attacked from astern again and scored a lucky hit near the 3in AA gun with his last bomb. The spreading fire soon detonated some of the ready-use ammunition, which caused the blaze to rage out of control. With his bombs expended and one engine knocked out, Jope reported the burning ship's position and headed for home. Shortly after Jope departed, the passengers and crew were forced to abandon the vessel. Later, British escorts arrived to try to tow the smoldering hulk back to port, but U-32 finished the liner off on October 28. The *Empress of Britain* was the largest British vessel sunk to date and her vulnerability to air attack shocked the Admiralty.

Jope's attack also convinced the Luftwaffe leadership that the Fw 200 was capable of more than just armed reconnaissance. On October 27, a lone Fw 200 attacked convoy OB 234 west of Ireland. Despite the presence of nine escort vessels, a Condor succeeded in damaging the 5,013-ton vessel *Alfred Jones*. An RAF Hudson from 224 Squadron based at Aldergrove in Northern Ireland arrived on the scene but when it attempted to interfere with the Condor attack, the Fw 200's gunners riddled it with 7.92mm fire.

The damaged Hudson managed to make it back to Aldergrove, but this was a rare air-to-air victory for the Condor. The British claimed that the destroyer HMS *Amazon* damaged the Condor with its 40mm "pom-pom" gun, but the attacker made it back to Bordeaux to report on the feebleness of British convoy defenses against low-level air strikes. This attack was the first time that a Condor deliberately targeted a convoy.

In November, Petersen began to ramp up KG 40's operational tempo against lucrative targets off the northwest coast of Ireland. On November 4, a single Fw 200 found the unescorted 19,141-ton liner *Windsor Castle* 290km (180 miles) west of Ireland. The ship's two Lewis gunners were alert and managed to drive off the first couple of bombing runs, but finally the Condor managed to drop a 250kg bomb squarely amidships that penetrated the superstructure. The bomb failed to detonate and was later disarmed. On November 9, another KG 40 Condor found the 26,032-ton liner *Empress of Japan* 282km (175 miles) west of Ireland and executed a perfect low-level attack from astern. Two 250kg bombs hit the stern but bounced off before exploding, causing only superficial damage. Around 1000hrs on November 15, a Condor found the inbound convoy SL 53, which had a particularly weak escort of one elderly destroyer and a single AMC. The Condor singled out the 9,333-ton passenger steamer *Apapa* and boldly executed a "Swedish turnip" attack from the port side at a height of 50m, scoring one solid bomb hit which destroyed the engines and set the cargo on fire. The escorts succeeded in rescuing most of the passengers before the vessel broke in two and sank. All told, KG 40 was able to mount ten successful anti-shipping strikes in Irish waters in November that sank six ships and damaged seven.

These attacks in November, particularly the three attacks on large liners being used as troop transports, stunned the Admiralty. It was now clear that the Condor was, in fact,

An Allied diagram shows the armament and vulnerability of the Fw 200. British fighter tactics initially focused on trying to set the poorly-protected wing fuel tanks alight but attacks from astern offered a high probability of incurring damage from the A- or B-stand positions. By May 1941, the RAF recommended head-on attacks to kill the pilots. (Author's collection)

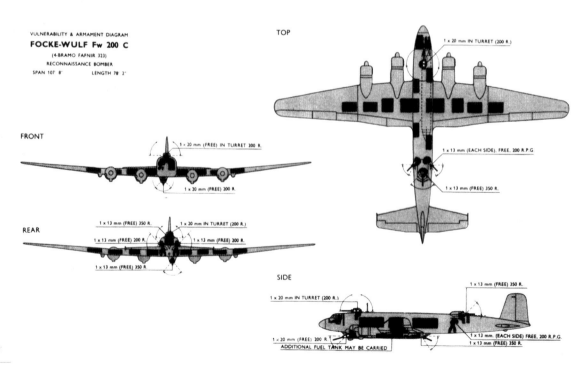

CONDOR ATTACK PROFILE

A typical KG 40 Condor sortie from Bordeaux-Merignac would see the crew arising around midnight, eating breakfast and then heading to a target briefing. Usually sorties were directed toward known convoy routes where either U-boats or the Kriegsmarine's *B-Dienst* (intelligence service) had detected recent traffic, although the information could be 12–24 hours old by the time the crew received it. Unlike a standard bomber mission against a fixed target, the Condor was assigned a search area where either moving convoys or independently steaming ships were expected to pass through. While the navigator plotted the appropriate course, the ground crews finished fueling and arming the plane. If more than one Fw 200 was involved in the mission, they would coordinate their search zones to cover the maximum amount of area near the suspected convoy. Between 0100 and 0200hrs, the aircraft would take off and head west toward the convoy routes. Usually the Condor would reach its search zone in about six hours, after a long boring flight over the Atlantic. In 1940–42 there was little or no risk of enemy interception on the outbound leg, but by 1943 aircrews had to be alert for enemy air activity over the Bay of Biscay. During the outbound leg, Condors flew in radio silence, even if operating with several aircraft.

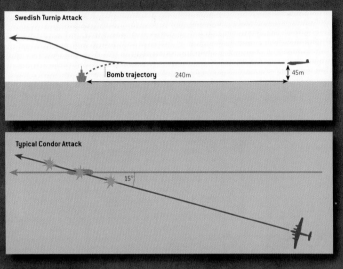

Finding convoys or independent ships proved to be far more difficult than Petersen expected. The combination of stale intelligence and poor long-range navigation skills over water led to many of the early Condor missions failing in their task. Convoys were usually difficult to spot, particularly in overcast winter weather over the Atlantic, with visibility often reduced to only a few miles. Once a Condor arrived in its target area, as many of the crew as possible would use binoculars to scan the sea for shipping while the pilot flew several search legs through the zone. If multiple aircraft were involved in the mission, they would split up at this point to cover their individual areas. Typical endurance in the search area was initially about three to four hours, but this was extended as improved Fw 200 models arrived in 1941–42.

If a convoy or other significant target was spotted by the observers, the pilot would usually maneuver in closer, using clouds for concealment as much as possible, and observe the target for a while. The *bordfunker* would break radio silence to vector in other Condors if they were nearby, so as to mount a coordinated attack. During this observation phase, which could last up to an hour, the crew would try to identify the escorts, if any, as well as

the best targets to attack. Ideally, the Fw 200 sought its victims from stragglers or "tail-end Charlies," minimizing the risk of defensive fire. Since the early Condors lacked an effective bombsight, strikes were only possible at low-level. Martin Harlinghausen had developed the "Swedish turnip" attack method with X.*Fliegerkorps*, which entailed approaching the target from abeam at a height of 45–50m and then releasing the bombs about 300–400m short of the target. Ideally, the bombs would glide into the target, striking at the waterline. This method offered a high probability of a hit, but also exposed the attacking aircraft to the vessel's AA guns (if it was equipped with any). KG 40 used the "Swedish turnip" extensively in 1940–41 but many pilots preferred the safer approach of attacking from dead astern. From that angle the chances of a hit were reduced, but it was safer for the Condor as the DEMS ships normally carried their anti-aircraft guns toward the bow. Just in case, most Fw 200s would use their ventral machine guns or 20mm cannon to strafe the decks, in order to suppress any flak gunners.

Normally a Condor would make several passes on a target, dropping only one or two bombs each time. As it overflew, hopefully not taking too much AA fire, the pilot would pull up sharply and turn around for another pass, or if the first attack was successful, shift to another target. Once all bombs were expended, the Condor would depart, heading back to either Bordeaux, or to Værnes in Norway. From Værnes, it would return to Bordeaux via Bremen, giving Focke-Wulf the chance to repair any damage or mechanical defects. With an individual aircraft usually taking anything from a few days to a week to do the entire return cycle, this system further reduced the operational sortie rate, but helped keep the available Condors in satisfactory shape.

a real threat to British shipping in its own right. The Admiralty asked RAF Coastal Command to reinforce the single Hudson squadron at Aldergrove with more and better aircraft, but Coastal Command, which was preoccupied with a variety of other priorities at the time, only transferred 272 Squadron with Bristol Blenheim IVs to beef up convoy escorts. This hapless unit had difficulty finding the convoys it was supposed to protect as well as distinguishing between enemy and friendly aircraft, and on November 24, one of its Blenheims engaged in a dogfight with an FAA Fairey Fulmar, fortunately without loss. On November 30, two Blenheims from Aldergrove managed to spot an Fw 200 near the Irish coast but lost it in cloud cover before they could intercept. It is fair to say that RAF Coastal Command did not bother KG 40 operations much in 1940.

Petersen was unable to maintain this operational tempo in December and poor weather limited the ability to spot targets. Nevertheless, at around 1100hrs on December 3, a Condor detected convoy HX 90 as it approached the Irish coast, and despite the presence of four escorts, the aircraft boldly flew between the fourth and fifth columns to bomb one cargo ship and strafe another. Turning around, the Condor attacked the cargo ship *W. Hendrik* and scored a direct hit, which according to the convoy commodore's report produced a "terrific explosion and [the] ship [was] wreathed in flames for a few seconds." During December, KG 40 sank three ships and damaged seven others, while only four Condors had been lost since the beginning of the blockade in August. By Christmas, KG 40 had sunk 19 ships of 100,000 tons and damaged 37 ships of 180,000 tons, while British convoy defenses had failed to destroy a single Condor. The first round in this duel had clearly gone to the Luftwaffe, which provoked Churchill to dub the Fw 200 "the scourge of the Atlantic." KG 40 now had enough trained crews and new aircraft to form two complete operational *staffeln* of six Condors each. It was also over New Year that the Kriegsmarine temporarily gained tactical control over KG 40.

Rested over the holidays with home leave in Germany, KG 40's crews returned with a vengeance on January 8, 1941, when they attacked the 6,278-ton cargo ship *Clytoneus* near Rockall and scored a direct hit that split the unfortunate vessel wide open. Three days later, an Fw 200 sank a straggler from convoy HG 49 west of Ireland, and on January 16, a Condor flown by Hauptmann Konrad Verlohr, the commander of 1.*Staffel*, spotted convoy OB 274. Its 40 merchant ships were protected by an unusually strong escort with three destroyers and three Flower class corvettes, but Verlohr executed two perfect "Swedish turnip" attacks that sank two freighters. Unlike most Condor pilots who would head for home after successful attacks, Verlohr stayed to shadow the convoy, radioing its position to nearby U-boats, but none were able to reach it before he had to depart. Petersen began to alternate his two *staffeln* so that he could increase KG 40's sorties, and when convoys HG 50 and SL 61 were spotted west of Ireland on January 19, he was able to attack them five days in a row, resulting in the destruction of seven ships. Again and again, KG 40 exploited the feebleness of the Royal Navy's low-level air defenses and RAF Coastal Command's failure to provide effective air cover, enabling it to savage one convoy after another. Churchill was incensed by the ease with which the Condors were able to swoop in and claim victims, even in the face of Royal Navy escorts.

The slaughter continued in the last week of January 1941, with repeated attacks on the next convoy, SL 62. One attack scored five bomb hits on the Norwegian freighter *Austvard* and used pinpoint cannon fire to destroy its radio shack. By the end of January, the surge in Condor attacks had sunk 17 ships of 65,000 tons and damaged five others. In return, the British had destroyed only a single Condor – the Fw 200 C-3 flown by Oberleutnant Burmeister – who incautiously decided to conduct a low-level strafing run on the rescue tugboat HMS *Seaman* on January 10. Although only 369 tons, the *Seaman* was extremely well armed against low-level attack with one of the few available 20mm Oerlikon guns, a 12-pdr and two .50cal machine guns. Burmeister was surprised to run into a wall of intense flak that holed his plane and forced him to ditch near the tugboat. He and two other survivors of the crew were captured and revealed under interrogation a great deal about Condor operations, which allowed the British to begin developing effective countermeasures. The tiny tugboat *Seaman* had not only struck the first blow against the Condor, but it had accomplished what larger warships had failed to do, and thereby set the Royal Navy upon the path to reversing the Condor's ascendancy.

If January was bad for the British, February 1941 was worse. KG 40 continued to pick off individual merchant ships west of Ireland with single-plane sorties but on February 9, Peterson shifted tactics and area of operations. He sent five Fw 200s, flown by the best pilots in the group, against convoy HG 53, which had been detected by U-boats southwest of Portugal. Aside from a few two-plane sorties, KG 40 had not previously launched multi-plane strikes against a single convoy and this attack caught the British by surprise. The Condors only sank five small ships totaling 9,201 tons, but they caused the convoy to scatter so badly that U-37 was able to slip in and sink three more. This was the classic joint attack that Dönitz had envisioned when he lobbied for the Fw 200 and it proved devastating in practice. Of some consolation was the fact that .50cal AA fire from the sloop HMS *Deptford* had punctured the fuel tank of the Fw 200 C-1 flown by Oberleutnant Erich Adam, who managed to reach the coast before crashing the aircraft in an olive grove in Moura, Portugal.

Dönitz also wanted the Condors to find convoys for his U-boats and shadow them until his wolfpacks could assemble, but this proved more difficult. Typically, KG 40 mounted only one long-range maritime reconnaissance sortie per day and even if it found a convoy, it could usually only shadow it for three to four hours, whereas it might take anything between 12 and 24 hours for U-boats to arrive. Convoy OB 287 was spotted by KG 40 northwest of Ireland on February 19 and endured three days of single-plane attacks that sank two freighters and damaged three more, but U-96 arrived only in time to finish off one of the cripples. Finally, on February 22, a Condor shadowed convoy OB 288 long enough to guide U-boats toward it and they succeeded in sinking nine ships of 42,282 tons. Petersen mounted another multi-plane attack against OB 290 on February 26, with four Fw 200s. Despite the presence of seven escorts, the Condors sank seven ships of 35,107 tons and so disorganized the convoy that U-47, commanded by the legendary Günther Prien, was able to penetrate the screen and sink three more. The Kriegsmarine was quite pleased with the success of KG 40's Condors in February, which had not only managed to sink 21 ships of 84,301

Condor attacks on British shipping, 1940–41.

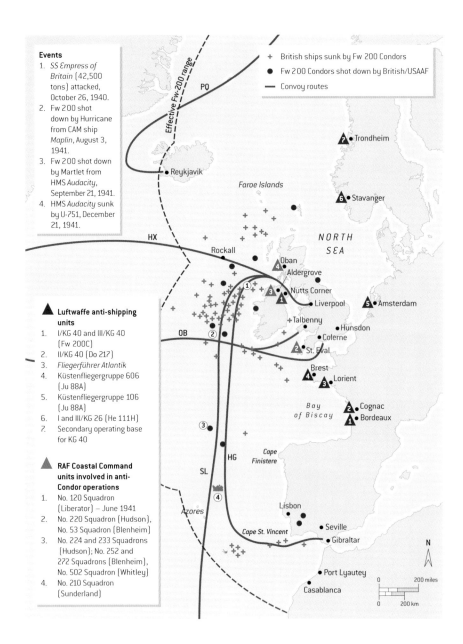

Events

1. *SS Empress of Britain* (42,500 tons) attacked, October 26, 1940.
2. Fw 200 shot down by Hurricane from CAM ship *Maplin*, August 3, 1941.
3. Fw 200 shot down by Martlet from HMS *Audacity*, September 21, 1941.
4. HMS *Audacity* sunk by U-751, December 21, 1941.

+ British ships sunk by Fw 200 Condors
● Fw 200 Condors shot down by British/USAAF
— Convoy routes

▲ Luftwaffe anti-shipping units

1. I/KG 40 and III/KG 40 (Fw 200C)
2. II/KG 40 (Do 217)
3. *Fliegerführer Atlantik*
4. Küstenfliegergruppe 606 (Ju 88A)
5. Küstenfliegergruppe 106 (Ju 88A)
6. I and III/KG 26 (He 111H)
7. Secondary operating base for KG 40

▲ RAF Coastal Command units involved in anti-Condor operations

1. No. 120 Squadron (Liberator) – June 1941
2. No. 220 Squadron (Hudson), No. 53 Squadron (Blenheim)
3. No. 224 and 233 Squadrons (Hudson); No. 252 and 272 Squadrons (Blenheim), No. 502 Squadron (Whitley)
4. No. 210 Squadron (Sunderland)

tons, but had also improved the lethal nature of wolfpack tactics by introducing a new combat dynamic – daylight air attacks to scatter the convoy, followed up by massed U-boat night attacks. Despite the promise these tactics held for winning the Battle of the Atlantic, the Condors had in fact already reached their high-water mark.

In March, the Luftwaffe regained control over KG 40 and put it under Martin Harlinghausen as *Fliegerführer Atlantik*. Petersen was unable to sustain the high sortie rates of January and February and virtually suspended operations for two weeks. He then returned to single-plane sorties, which found few convoys but managed to sink three ships and damage two more. Efforts to mount a coordinated Fw 200 and U-boat attack on convoy OB 302 on March 30–31 failed, as neither could find the

German propaganda photo of a Condor crew receiving a pre-mission brief in 1941. During the winter of 1940–41, KG 40 's exploits against British shipping helped to restore some of the Luftwaffe's luster after their failure to defeat the RAF in the summer of 1940. (Author's collection)

target. In April, Petersen was able to ramp back up to 74 sorties during the month, with major attacks on the 6th and the 16th and by the end of the month the group had sunk seven ships. However, KG 40 lost seven Condors in April, including three destroyed on the ground at Bordeaux by an RAF raid. More ominously, RAF Coastal Command finally succeeded in intercepting an Fw 200 C-3 off western Ireland on April 16, using a Beaufighter from Aldergrove, indicating that the British were finally getting serious about establishing anti-Condor patrols. Another Condor that attacked convoy HG 58 on April 18 was so damaged by AA fire that it crashed in Ireland.

Although KG 40 made a major effort in May to find Allied convoys and guide U-boats toward them, it failed on each occasion, beginning with a four-day effort against OB 316. Despite one or more Condor sorties each day, KG 40 lost contact before the nearest U-boats could arrive and the 20 ships of OB 316 made it to their destinations unscathed. Dönitz became so frustrated with the inability of KG 40 to find and then shadow convoys effectively that he decided to shift his operations further westward and not rely on the Condor. He was instantly rewarded when four of his U-boats found the unescorted convoy OB 318 on May 7 and sank nine of its ships over a period of three days. Nevertheless, KG 40 continued to try and work with the U-boats but botched shadowing efforts against HX 122. It enjoyed minor success in finding SL 72 on May 11 and OB 321 on May 14, sinking one ship from each convoy, but it again failed to guide any U-boats to the target. British low-level defenses were noticeably improving, which limited KG 40's victories in May to only three ships sunk and one damaged. More Condors were being damaged by AA fire and on May 19, Oberleutnant Hans Buchholz, the commander of 1. *Staffel* and a *Ritterkreuz* recipient, was shot down by AA machine gun fire from the freighter *Umgeni* west of Ireland. Buchholz was killed but the freighter rescued the rest of his crew.

When convoy HG 65 was located 350km off the Portuguese coast on June 15, Petersen dispatched another massed sortie of five Condors, hoping to repeat earlier successes. This time, however, the British were better prepared to deal with low-level air attacks and had developed new tactics. Instead of remaining in front of the convoy to ward off U-boats, the five escorts pulled back to form a tight defensive screen around the merchant ships and the sloop HMS *Wellington* positioned itself in the center. The first Fw 200 strike began at 0650hrs but failed to achieve any hits. More Condors joined in, strafing the decks of both merchant ships and warships, but the escort commander moved the corvette HMS *Geranium* to the rear of the group to disrupt further Condor attacks from astern, and ordered *Wellington* to keep them at bay with its 3in high-angle gun. Nevertheless, the Condors attacked again and again and the commodore wrote:

> 5 or 6 separate aircraft attacks were made at a level of not more than 200 feet, flying between the lines of the convoy at an even lower level. 2 of the Focke Wolfe's were seen to have been hit by several bursts of *Wellington*'s .5 machine guns, possibly also by the Lewis guns, but no hits could be claimed for certain by the 3" H.A. gun, though on two occasions the aircraft sheered off and abandoned their attack when fired upon by this gun. All the escorts claimed to have hit 1 or more of the planes several times, and they were also damaged by fire from the convoy itself.
>
> The "almost complete failure of the attacks" was attributed to the fact that "the convoy and escorts kept well together so that the maximum fire power could be developed, and aircraft were never left unfired at when within range".[3]

Although still poorly armed, the merchantmen in convoy HG 65 fired back with everything they had, ranging from rifles to Hotchkiss and Lewis AA machine guns to a Holman projector. The British noted that the Condor attacks were persistent but not well coordinated, for the ships were allowed to fend off single-plane strikes when they might have been overwhelmed by simultaneous multi-axis assaults. A British Catalina flying boat arrived and sparred with one of the Condors, but otherwise kept its distance. After several hours of attack, the five Condors had scored no direct hits and headed for home empty-handed. Worse still, one Fw 200 C-3 was so badly damaged by .50cal fire that it crash-landed in Portugal while another was forced to land in Spain. The Spanish allowed the Germans to fly in repair parts and technicians, enabling the damaged Condor to eventually fly back to Bordeaux. The attack on HG 65 was a disaster for KG 40 and a clear indication that British convoy defenses were evolving to deal with the Condor. Even more embarrassingly, another effort against convoy OG 66 was aborted after a series of mishaps. The Condor that spotted the shipping misreported the location by 122km so that when three more Fw 200s were sent to attack the convoy, they failed to find it and one of them disappeared over the ocean. By the end of June, KG 40 had sunk only four small ships totaling less than 6,000 tons but had lost four Fw 200s.

---

3   HMS *Wellington*'s Report of Proceedings, June 29, 1941.

THE TEST OF STRENGTH, JULY–DECEMBER 1941

In the post-action review following the attack on convoy HG 65, Harlinghausen ordered that Condors would no longer use the "Swedish turnip" attack method since they were too vulnerable to improved British shipboard defenses. Thus in July 1941, KG 40 shifted entirely to the maritime reconnaissance role and only authorized anti-shipping attacks against lone vessels. Condors succeeded in locating four convoys for the U-boats in July but they sank no ships themselves. Hauptmann Fritz Fliegel, a *Ritterkreuz* recipient who had just been given command of I/KG 40, decided to try his luck against convoy OB 346 on July 18, and attacked the 7,046-ton freighter *Pilar de Larrinaga*. However, the gunners on the freighter scored a lucky 12-pdr hit on Fliegel's starboard wing, which tore it off. Fliegel spiraled out of control into the sea – the end of the career of another KG 40 ace. The convoy also included the FCS ship SS *Maplin*, which became the first of its kind to launch a "Hurricat" fighter at sea, flown by Lieutenant Bob Everett. On this occasion, by the time that Everett was airborne, Fliegel had already been splashed. Convoy shadowing was not an entirely safe enterprise either, as another Fw 200 C-3 found on July 23 when it was intercepted 400km (250 miles) west of Ireland by a Lockheed Hudson from 233 Squadron. The Hudson promptly shot down the Condor, although the crew members were subsequently picked up. In total, four Condors were lost in July.

On August 2, a Condor spotted the 20-ship convoy SL 81 west of Ireland and began a concerted shadowing effort to guide in several U-boats. However, SL 81 was accompanied not only by Escort Group 7 with 11 warships, but the FCS ship SS *Maplin*, which now got another crack at the Condors. On the afternoon of August 3, a Condor flown by Unteroffizier Hasek appeared and began to shadow the convoy and the *Maplin* launched its Sea Hurricane fighter, again flown by Lieutenant Bob Everett. Hasek and his crew did not see the plume of smoke from the rocket catapult launch and Everett was able to close on the unsuspecting Fw 200 from the rear. Everett made three attacks from behind which caused large fragments of the aircraft's exterior fuselage to break off. The Condor's defensive fire was inaccurate, allowing Everett to keep hammering the target until it caught fire and crashed into the sea. Satisfied with his victory, Everett succeeded in ditching his Sea Hurricane near the convoy rescue ship, thereby validating the concept of the catapult ship. KG 40 gained some revenge the next day when another Fw 200 swooped in and sank a 4,337-ton freighter, followed by a devastating U-boat attack on August 5 that sank five ships from the convoy. KG 40 operations were also impacted by the diversion of six Fw 200s under Major Petersen to the Mediterranean to conduct anti-shipping attacks in the Suez Canal area.

The appearance of catapult ships and improved anti-air defensive tactics were indicators that the duel between the Fw 200 and the Allied convoys was turning against the Germans, but KG 40 continued to mount long-range reconnaissance operations west of Ireland in September. Two separate battles developed on the Gibraltar route in late September, involving convoys HG 73 and OG 74. Condors

OVERLEAF:
Convoy HG 53 left Gibraltar on the afternoon of February 6, 1941, bound for Liverpool with 19 merchant ships escorted by the destroyer HMS *Velox* and the sloop HMS *Deptford*. U-37 spotted the convoy and attacked at 0440 hours on 9 February, sinking two ships. The U-boat captain reported the sighting, which was relayed to KG 40 in Bordeaux. Rather than sending one or two Condors as usual, KG 40 launched its first mass attack against a convoy with five Condors, led by Hauptmann Fritz Fliegel. They found the convoy 400 miles southwest of Lisbon around 1600 hours. One Condor quickly scored hits on the 2,490-ton steamer *Britannic*, which sank in minutes. As the Condors began another run, the convoy opened fire with every available gun and HMS *Deptford* was able to damage the wing of Oberleutnant Erich Adam's Condor. Adam managed to complete his bombing run but had to land in Spain due to the loss of fuel. Nevertheless, the four remaining Condors flown by Fliegel, Buchholz, Jope and Schlosser sank four more steamers, throwing the convoy into total chaos. Here, Schlosser has just turned away after hitting the *Britannic*, while Adam is beginning his bomb run on the 1,759-ton steamer *Jura*. This day turned out to be one of the best executed attacks on a convoy by KG 40 and was an ominous indicator to the British Admiralty of the need to rapidly develop new weapons and tactics to deal with this type of low-level threat.

53

Oberfeldwebel Heinrich
Bleichert attempted to
shadow convoy OG 69
some 400km (250 miles)
west of Ireland on July 23,
1941, when it was intercepted
by an RAF Lockheed Hudson
Mk V from 233 Squadron.
After a brief aerial combat
Bleichert's Fw 200 C-3 was
shot down, but 7 seven of
8 the eight crew members
survived and were captured.
(Imperial War Museum
C 1988)

detected HG 73 first and found that it consisted of 25 merchantmen and 11 escorts, including the catapult ship HMS *Springbank*. On September 18, *Springbank* launched its single Fulmar against a shadowing Condor but although the British fighter got close enough to engage, its machine guns quickly jammed due to faulty ammunition. After its Fulmar was expended the convoy was without air cover and the Condors returned and began to guide in four U-boats. The U-boats savaged convoy HG 73, sinking ten ships of 25,818 tons, including *Springbank*. Almost simultaneously, the battle against convoy OG 74 began. This convoy had 26 merchantmen and ten escorts, including the first escort carrier to be built, HMS *Audacity*. On the morning of September 21, an Fw 200 C-3 caught the rescue ship *Walmer Castle* behind the convoy as it was picking up survivors from a U-boat attack, and quickly sank it with two bombs. The attack alerted the combat air patrol of two Martlet fighters flown by Sub-Lieutenant Norris Patterson and Sub-Lieutenant Graham Fletcher from *Audacity*, which suddenly appeared and engaged the Condor:

> Pat came in from the quarter raking the Kurier all the way as he slid into the astern position. He had just broken away to avoid colliding with her when Fletch let blast with a full deflection shot from dead abeam. Only thirty-five rounds were fired from each of his four guns, but the Kurier's entire tail unit fell off.[4]

After this victory, the Condors kept their distance from OG 74. Although the Condors were becoming better at finding convoys for U-boats, their ability to attack or even shadow convoys was deteriorating rapidly in the face of improved British defenses. It was also a time for change in KG 40 as Oberstleutnant Georg Pasewaldt took over from the departed Petersen. Poor weather severely limited KG 40 operations in October and although the Condors were able to shadow convoy OG 75 for almost eight days, the strong escort was able to limit losses to only a single vessel. HMS *Audacity* escorted convoy HG 74 from Gibraltar to Liverpool without loss.

On October 28, HMS *Audacity*, with eight Martlet fighters embarked, left Liverpool with convoy OG 76 bound for Gibraltar. KG 40 did not detect them until November 6, but then committed six Fw 200s to provide a sustained shadowing effort

4   Brown, Eric, *Wings on My Sleeve*, London, Orion (2006), p.26.

in order for a large wolfpack to intercept the convoy. When British shipboard radar detected a Condor approaching on November 8, the commander of 802 Squadron, Lieutenant-Commander John Wintour, took off to intercept. Wintour made two regulation attacks from astern that set the Condor on fire but then incautiously pulled up abreast of his damaged opponent, allowing the German dorsal gunner to pour a stream of 20mm fire into his cockpit. Once Wintour was killed, his wingman pounced on the burning Fw 200 and unceremoniously destroyed it. The Condor had proved very vulnerable to fighter attack but it had also demonstrated that it was not to be trifled with. Later that day, more intruders were detected and HMS *Audacity* launched Lieutenant Eric Brown and his flight commander, Lieutenant-Commander Peter "Sheepy" Lamb to deal with two Fw 200s approaching the convoy:

We were then at 4,000 feet. There was the Focke-Wulf below us at about 800 feet. I heard Sheepy call, "I see another one," and then, "You take the low one, I'll take this one."

I came in on my bandit in a diving attack from the port beam, but the deflection was too much and my closing speed so high that I only got in a one-second burst before I had to break away underneath him. There was no return fire. I had caught him unawares. As I passed under him I started to maneuver myself into position for a starboard quarter attack, determined that this was going to be one from the book. It still only allowed me about a two-second burst but set his starboard inner engine alight, although he was now taking evasive action.

I came round again for another port-beam attack. Again I could only get off a one-second burst. I was being cramped in setting up my attacks by the low cloud layer and by him turning into me. On breaking away I saw the Kurier head into this covering layer as I darted after him and was soon through its 400-feet depth, but without any sign of my prey.

I stayed on top because the cloud was broken and I hoped I might see him again. Suddenly I spotted a wingtip just poking through the cotton wool. He was turning and finding it difficult to keep his 100-odd feet of wingspan tucked away in the thinning cloud. Twice I got these glimpses of him, but he eluded me.

A British souvenir cover commemorating the first shooting-down of an Fw 200 C-3 Condor by Martlet fighters from HMS *Audacity*, which actually occurred on 21 September 1941. This victory was achieved by Sub-Lieutenant Graham Fletcher. He was shot down and killed by flak from U-131 on December 17, 1941. (Author's collection)

The 4,337-ton freighter *Tunisia*, sunk west of Ireland on August 4, 1941. Ships sailing independently like this were easy pickings for Condor attacks. (Author's collection)

HMS *Audacity* with six Martlet fighters on deck, late 1941. The lack of an elevator meant that all maintenance had to be carried out on deck and the aircraft were constantly exposed to the elements.. (Author's collection)

I was in despair at the cat-and-mouse game when he appeared where I least expected him, about 500 yards dead ahead of me. I had no time to think. I just blazed away at him as we rushed on to what looked like inevitable collision. I knew that if I missed this time I would never see him again, so I held on till the last possible second. It was close enough to see the big windscreen round the two German pilots shatter. As debris flew off its nose I took violent evading action to avoid a collision. I felt sure I must have killed both pilots.

The huge machine reared, stalled, and spiraled flatly into the sea. The port wing broke off on impact. I circled over the crash and to my surprise saw two men crawl out of an escape hatch on top of the fuselage. As the aircraft filled with water and sank they clung to the broken wing, which still floated.[5]

Brown had shot down Oberleutnant Karl Krüger and had discovered that the Fw 200 was particularly vulnerable to head-on attacks. Thanks to HMS *Audacity*'s air cover, neither the U-boats nor the Condors could lay a hand on convoy OG 76, which made it through to Gibraltar unscathed. After a brief stopover, HMS *Audacity* began the return trip to Liverpool with convoy HG 76 on December 14. By noon on December 16, Condors had spotted them and began guiding in the five U-boats of the "*Seeräuber*" wolfpack. However, the British escort group under Commander F. J. Walker was unusually aggressive and succeeded in keeping the U-boats at bay, while HMS *Audacity*'s four remaining Martlets went after the Fw 200s. The Martlets chased off two Condors on December 18, but had more success the next day when Lieutenant Brown shot down his second Condor with another head-on attack and Lieutenant-Commander James Sleigh repeated this tactic against a Condor in the late afternoon. After the loss of three Condors to HMS *Audacity*'s fighters, KG 40's Fw 200s kept their distance but the U-boats were finally able to penetrate Walker's screen and sank a destroyer and two merchant ships. On the evening of December 21,

5   Brown, *Wings on My Sleeve*, pp.29–30.

U-751 managed to spot HMS *Audacity* outside the convoy and hit it with three torpedoes. The escort carrier sank in just ten minutes but five of the six fighter pilots from 802 Squadron survived. With HMS *Audacity* gone, a Condor returned to shadow the convoy the next morning, despite the presence of an RAF Liberator.

The last six months of 1941 had proved a severe blow to KG 40. Only four ships of 10,298 tons had been sunk in anti-shipping operations with two more damaged, whereas 16 Condors had been lost, including seven shot down by convoy defenses. Although the Condors had enjoyed some success in guiding U-boats toward convoys, it was clear that the days of easy low-level air attacks were over and that the duel for supremacy over Britain's lifelines had turned against the Germans. On the British side, the CAM ships had been marginally useful but HMS *Audacity* had fully vindicated the concept of the escort carrier for convoy defense, which was now enthusiastically embraced by the Admiralty.

RELEGATED TO THE SIDELINES

In the face of ever-stronger convoy defenses, and not yet equipped with a suitable bombsight to enable higher-level attacks, the Fw 200 Condors were withdrawn from anti-shipping operations in 1942 and reverted to their original role of providing long-range maritime reconnaissance. Yet even in this task they were being increasingly relegated to the sidelines. As the year began, the Battle of the Atlantic was shifting from the focus on severing British supply lines to a wider global campaign. With the United States in the war, Dönitz decided to reallocate as many U-boats as possible to attack the weakly defended American shipping, which effectively moved the main U-boat campaign beyond the range of Fw 200 support. In the first three months of 1942, KG 40 continued to shadow a few convoys approaching Great Britain but with poor

A Fleet Air Arm Grumman Martlet fighter. This American-built aircraft was originally designated for the French Navy but was diverted to British service in July 1940. Its six .50cal machine guns proved lethal to the Condors. (Author's collection)

results. On January 2, an RAF Beaufighter shot down a Condor off the northwest Spanish coast, indicating that the route across the Bay of Biscay was no longer risk-free. A detachment of six Ju 88Cs was sent to Bordeaux to provide long-range escorts for the Condors, offering a temporary respite from RAF predators.

While Dönitz was sending his main U-boat force westward, Hitler ordered the Kriegsmarine and Luftwaffe to concentrate their forces in northern Norway to counter the British convoys running between Reykjavik and Murmansk. In March, it was decided to send Major Edmund Daser's I/KG 40 to Værnes airfield near Trondheim to provide long-range reconnaissance for *Luftflotte* 5 against the Arctic convoys. Major Robert Kowalewski's III/KG 40, which was still converting from He 111s to Fw 200s, would remain at Bordeaux and continue to operate against the Gibraltar convoys. *Fliegerführer Atlantik* was stripped to the bone to provide anti-shipping units for Norway, which effectively brought the aerial blockade of Great Britain to an abrupt end.

In Norway, I/KG 40 had begun operating against the Russian convoys in May 1942 when a Condor spotted PQ 16. In July, a Condor spotted PQ 17 and I/KG 40 participated in the shadowing effort, which cost it an Fw 200. At no point did the Condors engage in anti-shipping attacks against these convoys, leaving that role to the He 111s of KG 26 and the Ju 88s of KG 30. Daser was also ordered to send many of his aircraft on long-range reconnaissance sorties as far west as Iceland to try to spot the British convoys as they left Reykjavik. The US Army Air Force (USAAF) had already brought fighters to defend Iceland's airspace by the time that I/KG 40 began reconnaissance flights around Reykjavik, and Daser's Condors soon ran into trouble. On August 14, 1942, two USAAF P-39 fighters shot down an Fw 200 C-4 that was scouting shipping around Reykjavik and USAAF fighters claimed another Condor on October 24. A number of Fw 200s simply disappeared on the long Atlantic flights, probably falling victim to catastrophic mechanical failure. All told, Daser's I/KG 40 lost 12 Condors to enemy action in 1942 and 15 to other causes. In return, KG 40 played little more than a minor supporting role in the campaign against the Arctic convoys. In October 1942, Daser's *gruppe* received six of the new He 177 *Greif* bombers, which were intended to replace the Fw 200, but technical problems continued to delay their operational debut. Nevertheless, OKL was beginning to regard the Fw 200 as no longer a front-line combat aircraft and in late November, I/KG 40 was forced to send all 18 of its Fw 200s to participate in the Stalingrad airlift (as KG zbv 200), in which nine of these aircraft were lost.

At Bordeaux, III/KG 40 focused on training until May 1942, when it began limited operations against the Gibraltar convoys. On May 1, an Fw 200 approaching a convoy west of Portugal found out the hard way that the superb 40mm Bofors anti-aircraft gun was beginning to reach the Royal Navy, when it was holed by fire from the ASW trawler HMS *Imperialist*. This Condor was able to reach the Portuguese coast before it crash-landed on a beach. The Portuguese repatriated the German aircrew but allowed British officials to retrieve documents from the wreck. CAM ships were also becoming more widespread on the Gibraltar route and a Sea Hurricane from the *Empire Heath* in convoy HG 91 shot down a shadowing Fw 200 on November 1,1942. Throughout 1942, III/KG 40 was little more than a minor nuisance to the Gibraltar convoys, at the cost of eight Condors lost to enemy action and seven to other causes. Between January and September 1942, only one of the 14 Gibraltar convoys was attacked and no ships were lost to air attack.

Based upon the results of operations to date, *Fliegerführer Atlantik* reported on December 3, 1942, that "because of inadequate armament, the Fw 200 is unfit for use in areas that are within range of land-based fighter planes. Confrontations between the Fw 200 and such fighters in medium cloud cover almost always lead to the destruction of the Fw 200. Further development of the Fw 200 cannot be recommended because its development has reached its limits and the aircraft should be replaced by the He 177."

While the Condors were sidelined in 1942, British convoy defenses improved considerably. The new escort carriers HMS *Biter* and HMS *Dasher* were active with the Gibraltar convoys by late 1942 and more CVEs would be joining the fleet in 1943. HMS *Avenger* had sailed on the Arctic run with PQ 18 and its Sea Hurricanes had shot down five German bombers before it was itself sunk by a U-boat on November 15, 1942. Nevertheless, Allied convoy defenses were firming up – particularly with the arrival of 20mm Oerlikon and 40mm Bofors guns on merchant ships – so that it appeared that the duel between the Condors and the convoys had been decided by the end of 1942. The enemy, however, always retains a vote in the conduct of war and KG 40 was not yet prepared to throw in the towel.

An American Lockheed P-38F Lightning fighter of the USAAF 50th Fighter Squadron based in Iceland. This unit destroyed one Condor on August 5, 1943, and helped to deter KG 40's long-range reconnaissance flights in the GIUK Gap area. (Library of Congress)

STRIKE AND COUNTERSTRIKE

During the last few months of 1942, III/KG 40 received 18 of the new Fw 200 C-4 bombers with the Lotfe 7D bombsight. With this aiming device, Condors could now conduct medium-altitude bombing missions that would reduce their vulnerability to much of the shipboard flak. The *Fliegerführer Atlantik* decided to use these improved Condors in a bold anti-shipping strike to counter the Allied build-up in North Africa. On the afternoon of December 31, 1942, a group of 11 Fw 200 C-4s took off from Bordeaux and headed southwest along the Portuguese coast. German intelligence had just detected the arrival of Allied troop convoy UGS 3 in the harbor at Casablanca and stationary shipping seemed to be an ideal target for the Condors. Distance to target was about 2,100km (1,250 miles), making this one of the longest bombing raids of the war. Three Condors aborted due to various problems, and although eight reached the port on New Year's Eve to drop thirty-two 250kg bombs among the shipping and docks, they achieved no significant hits. US Army flak units defending the port damaged one Fw 200 C-4, which crash-landed in the Canary Islands. Two other Condors ran out of fuel and landed in southern Spain where they were impounded. The raid on Casablanca achieved no significant results and cost III/KG 40 three aircraft, but it also signaled the beginning of the second phase in the duel between the Condor and Allied convoys.

In addition to the Lotfe 7D bombsight, a number of Condors were also beginning to receive rudimentary surface search radar, which dramatically improved their ability to find Allied shipping in the Atlantic. I/KG 40 remained in Norway but after the diversion of most its Fw 200s to the Stalingrad airlift, it began re-equipping with He 177 bombers and only operated small numbers of Condors in the maritime reconnaissance role in 1943. Instead, III/KG 40 was rebuilt as the primary Condor operator and it was reinforced to a strength of 40 Fw 200s by March 1943. *Fliegerführer Atlantik* decided to concentrate all the efforts of III/KG 40 against the Gibraltar convoys in order to disrupt the Allied build-up in the western Mediterranean.

Beginning in early March 1943, III/KG 40 tentatively renewed anti-shipping sorties off the Portuguese coast, between Lisbon and Cape St Vincent. This area was generally beyond the range of Allied fighters from Gibraltar and there were still too

An RAF Liberator from No. 120 Squadron based in Aldergrove, Northern Ireland, provides aerial escort to a convoy in April 1943. Once Coastal Command received adequate aircraft to protect shipping, the days of the Condor were numbered. (Imperial War Museum CH 9602)

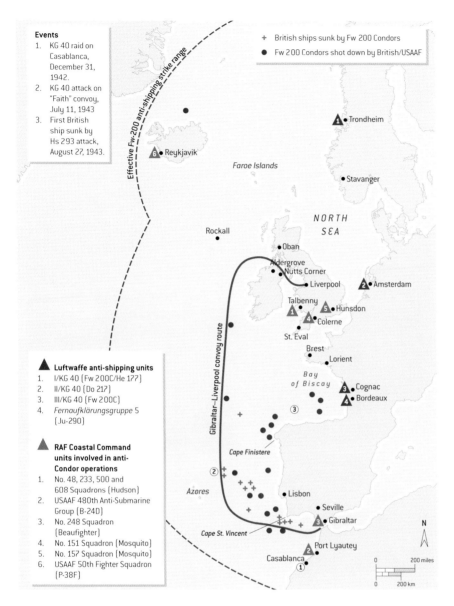

Events
1. KG 40 raid on Casablanca, December 31, 1942.
2. KG 40 attack on "Faith" convoy, July 11, 1943
3. First British ship sunk by Hs 293 attack, August 27, 1943.

+ British ships sunk by Fw 200 Condors
● Fw 200 Condors shot down by British/USAAF

Effective Fw-200 anti-shipping strike range

● Reykjavik

Faroe Islands

● Stavanger

▲ Trondheim

NORTH SEA

Rockall ●

● Oban
Aldergrove ● Nutts Corner
● Liverpool
▲ Amsterdam

Talbenny ● Hunsdon
● Colerne
St. Eval ●

Brest ●
● Lorient

Bay of Biscay
▲ Cognac
▲ Bordeaux

Gibraltar–Liverpool convoy route

Cape Finisterre

Azores

● Lisbon
● Seville
▲ Gibraltar

Cape St. Vincent

▲ Port Lyautey
Casablanca ●

N

0   200 miles
0   200 km

Luftwaffe anti-shipping units
1. I/KG 40 (Fw 200C/He 177)
2. II/KG 40 (Do 217)
3. III/KG 40 (Fw 200C)
4. *Fernaufklärungsgruppe 5* (Ju-290)

RAF Coastal Command units involved in anti-Condor operations
1. No. 48, 233, 500 and 608 Squadrons (Hudson)
2. USAAF 480th Anti-Submarine Group (B-24D)
3. No. 248 Squadron (Beaufighter)
4. No. 151 Squadron (Mosquito)
5. No. 157 Squadron (Mosquito)
6. USAAF 50th Fighter Squadron (P-38F)

few escort carriers available to provide air cover for more than a few convoys. However, two Condors were lost over the Bay of Biscay, including one shot down by an RAF Beaufighter. On March 19, 1943, an Fw 200 C-4 spotted convoy KMS 11 off the Portuguese coast but when it tried to attack, it was shot down by AA fire from the Free French sloop *Savorgnan de Brazza*. Undeterred, III/KG 40 attacked the same convoy two days later, and this time succeeded in sinking a 6,000-ton freighter – the first successful Condor attack on a convoy in over a year.

For some reason, III/KG 40 mounted no anti-shipping sorties in April 1943 but resumed action in May. On the evening of May 22, two Condors spotted a group of three Allied merchantmen off Cape St Vincent and attacked from medium altitude. Tom Scotland, who was a fireman aboard SS *Alpera*, recalled:

63

We arrived on deck just in time to see the two aircraft disappear into the setting sun, a favorite attacking position for aircraft. I stood right aft under the gun platform when I heard the gunlayer shout, "here they come!" then all hell let loose. How many bombs were dropped, I don't know but one entered the water and exploded just alongside the stern. The stern was lifted clear of the water and going up and down like a bucking bronco. I was hanging on to the taffrail with both hands to prevent myself from being thrown overboard. The guns of course were now silent, the gunners and the platform having been swamped by the deluge of water.

I saw the Captain on the bridge and he asked me to see what the position was in the engine room. The engines of course had stopped and I duly told him that water had risen above the deck plates and was pouring in all over the place. We heard that it was hoped to send a tug from Gibraltar to take us in tow. While I was talking to the Captain the aircraft returned and bombed us again, but this time the bombs dropped ahead of our ship, causing no more damage. However, the ship was slowly sinking and having brought everyone back on board, and discovering that there were only minor casualties we were forced to leave the vessel when only two or three feet of freeboard was left. The SS *Alpera* was taken in tow but foundered during the night.[6]

KG 40 repeated this tactic on May 30, attacking another small group of merchantmen off Cape St Vincent and sinking the 4,910-ton SS *Llancarvan*. In both attacks, the bombing accuracy was only sufficient to achieve near-misses that caused gradual flooding, rather than the kind of direct hits that were achieved with low-level strikes. Attacks continued on June 14 and 18, damaging two more ships, and a major assault was launched against convoy MKS 15 on June 23 that sank two vessels. However, when III/KG 40 tried this tactic against the small convoy XK 9 on June 24, it found that the British had brought in the new escort carrier HMS *Battler* for support. Radar detected the Condors' approach; *Battler's* two Seafire fighters on combat air patrol went tearing after the intruders and shot down an Fw 200 C-4. Adding to the reappearance of escort carriers on the Gibraltar run, RAF Coastal Command had recently received the superb Mosquito attack aircraft and began using them over the Bay of Biscay, where they shot down an Fw 200 C-4 in June. Additionally, four Coastal Command squadrons were redeployed to Gibraltar and the Lockheed Hudsons of 233 Squadron downed two Condors in the summer of 1943. The British also demonstrated superb inter-service cooperation by sending intercept teams of the RAF's Y-Service aboard British warships in the Bay of Biscay to monitor KG 40's radio communications, and the forward-based SIGINT provided vital early warning of Condor sorties.

On July 11, 1943, a group of Allied ships heading south was detected about 480km (300 miles) off the Portuguese coast. This was a special convoy known as "Faith," consisting of three large troopships escorted by two destroyers and a frigate. Three Condors attacked from medium altitude and this time achieved spectacular results with the Lotfe 7D bombsight. Both the 16,792-ton SS *California* and the 20,021-ton *Duchess of York* were hit and set on fire and were soon abandoned. The attack killed

6   Norman Date, "Tom Scotland" (Article A2619650), in BBC, *WW2 People's War*, London, BBC (2004).

more than 100 personnel aboard these two ships but 1,500 survivors were taken on board the remaining troopship, SS *Port Fairy*, which set off toward Gibraltar escorted by a single frigate. Two Condors spotted the *Port Fairy* and succeeded in hitting this ship as well before being driven off by two US Navy PBY Catalinas from Gibraltar. The attack on "Faith" was a shock to the British since the Condor threat had no longer been regarded as significant. Furthermore, the success of medium-altitude bombing with the Lotfe 7D emboldened KG 40 to renew attacks on larger convoys.

A reconnaissance sortie detected convoy OS 52KM about 370km (230 miles) northwest of Lisbon on July 26, and III/KG 40 promptly dispatched Condors to attack it. This was a particularly large convoy, with 68 merchant ships and eight escorts, including a Dido class light cruiser. The anti-aircraft armament carried by this convoy was impressive, with 56 of the merchantmen having at least one 20mm Oerlikon, adding up to a total of 198 Oerlikons. However, even this weaponry could not hit the Condors when they bombed from 3,000m, and KG 40 succeeded in sinking one freighter on July 26 and another on July 27. These strikes demonstrated that even very strong shipboard air defenses were not sufficient in themselves to counter the new form of Fw 200 attack.

Just as this battle ended, convoy SL133 was detected about 485km (300 miles) off Cape Finisterre. III/KG 40 sent two Condors to attack, unaware that the convoy had two CAM ships in its ranks. When the first Fw 200 appeared, the *Empire Darwin* launched Pilot Officer John Stewart in his Hurricane. Stewart got close enough to damage the Condor but his guns jammed – a frequent problem with aircraft exposed on deck to salt water for weeks at a time. Another Condor was soon spotted about 20km ahead of the convoy and the second CAM ship, *Empire Tide*, launched Pilot Officer Patrick Flynn to intercept the intruder. This action is recounted in Ralph Barker's *The Hurricats*:

Flynn climbed to 200 feet, and was able to engage with the Condor in a matter of minutes. Coming up astern of the Condor on the port quarter, Flynn opened fire with a two-second burst at 300 yards. There was a short burst from the port lateral machine gun of the Condor and as Flynn closed directly astern he saw that the gunners in the front and rear turrets were firing at him point blank...

Breaking off he executed a climbing turn into the sun, then began a series of beam and quarter attacks from the port side up sun. As with the other two Condors, the pilot took no violent evasive action but relied on his gunners. On his second run Flynn

concentrated his fire on the cockpit and knew he was on target, but he had to fly through blistering return fire and his Hurricane was repeatedly hit, mostly in the wings.

Even the impetuous Flynn realized that he would first have to silence the Condor's guns. Breaking off again, he began his third run by spraying the fuselage between the rear turret and the lateral gun position on the port side before closing to 100 yards and finishing up with a short burst of fire directed at the front turret. Again he saw his tracer stabbing its mark.

Having as he hoped silenced the gunners, he went now for the outer and inner port engines, but the answering fire was as withering as ever. The perspex of the cockpit hood behind his head suddenly splintered, and a gaping hole appeared in the port wing. For compensation he had to be content with increasing spurts of smoke from the Condor's port engines...

As he closed in for a final attack, a bomb from the Condor fell away right in front of him and he nearly flew into it. Soon afterwards he felt the blast from the explosion as it hit the sea. Then, as the Condor pilot jettisoned the rest of his bombs, Flynn fired a final burst that exhausted his ammunition.

He left the Condor pouring smoke and rapidly losing altitude. The combat had taken Flynn forty miles from the nearest ship. After 52 minutes in the air, Flynn managed to nurse his damaged aircraft to within sight of the Convoy before bailing out at 2,000 feet. Luckily, he only had to wait ten minutes in the water before being picked up by H.M.S. *Enchantress*, a convoy escort.[7]

Flynn had shot down an Fw 200 C-4, only the third and last Condor kill by a Hurricane from a CAM ship. However, III/KG 40 was not done with convoy SL 133 and now that the CAM ships had expended their single-shot fighters, decided to make a massed attack with seven Fw 200s the next day. Again using medium-altitude bombing, one Condor managed to hit the CAM ship *Empire Darwin* and set it on fire. The situation looked grim for the convoy until a British B-24 Liberator from No. 59 Squadron arrived and engaged the Condors:

When we arrived one ship was on fire and ships were being attacked by a Focke-Wulf 200 using high-level bombing technique. The senior naval officer of the convoy instructed us by radio to attack the enemy aircraft, which now numbered seven! We got on the tail of a Focke-Wulf which was going in to attack but the gunners on the ships let all hell loose. They fired at the Focke-Wulf 200 and ourselves but caused the enemy aircraft to swerve just as he was dropping his bombs. He missed his target altogether and to our amazement all seven Condors broke off the action and scurried for home.[8]

RAF Coastal Command was finally equipped with the right aircraft for the job – B-24 Liberators, Mosquitoes and Beaufighter Xs – that enabled it to mount long-range

7   Barker, Ralph, *Hurricats: The Fighters That Could Not Return,* Stroud, Tempus Publishing Ltd (2000), pp.153–54.
8   Bowman, Martin, *B-24 Liberator 1939–45,* Wellingborough, Patrick Stephens (1979), p. 66.

intruder operations in the Bay of Biscay and provide some measure of air cover for convoys. Between July 9 and August 2, 1943, Mosquitoes and Beaufighters shot down three Condors operating from Bordeaux. Adding to KG 40's discomfort, the USAAF's 480th Anti-Submarine Group, with two squadrons of B-24D Liberators, began operating from Port Lyautey in Morocco in June and aggressively patrolled the airspace off western Portugal. The first encounter between a B-24D and an Fw 200 C-5 occurred on July 31, and the Liberator succeeded in shooting down the Condor. Further action off Cape Finisterre on August 13 resulted in a damaged Fw 200 C-7 crash-landing in Spain, where it broke its back. Forgetting their anti-shipping mission, two Fw 200s attacked a single B-24D flown by Captain Hugh D. Maxwell Jr, on August 17. Maxwell's gunners succeeded in shooting down one Condor and damaging the other, but the Germans had knocked out two of his engines and he was forced to ditch. The damaged Fw 200 C-4 made it back to Bordeaux but was destroyed in a crash-landing. All told, the B-24Ds of the 480th Anti-Submarine Group engaged Condors seven times between July and October 1943, destroying four Condors. Although an unlikely candidate as an air superiority aircraft, the B-24D enjoyed a significant speed advantage over the lumbering Condor, packing greater firepower in its nose-mounted .50cal turret, and was able to take far more punishment.

The increased operations in June and July had cost III/KG 40 a total of 11 Condors and its strength was reduced to only nine operational aircraft by August 1. Yet when the southbound convoy OS 53 was located 355km (220 miles) northwest of Lisbon on August 15, the *gruppe* threw its remaining Condors against this target. OS 53 was not as strongly defended as previous convoys, having only the protection of a single ship armed with 20mm Oerlikons. The Condors succeeded in sinking a 6,070-ton freighter and damaging two others, but the sloop HMS *Stork* damaged an Fw 200 C-4, which was forced to land in Spain where it was then impounded. The attack on convoy OS 53 turned out to be the swan-song for the Condors in the duel against Atlantic convoys, since III/KG 40 lost a total of nine Condors in August 1943 and it no longer had the ability to continue sustained operations in the face of enemy air cover. Now that the He 177 bomber was finally approaching operational readiness, the Luftwaffe decided to wind down Fw 200 production and eventually convert all of KG 40 to the new bomber.

A few anti-shipping strikes continued off Portugal in September, but to add insult to injury, the tiny 471-ton Belgian coaster *René Paul* shot down an Fw 200 C-5 off Cape St Vincent on September 2. On September 13, a Condor spotted the 7,135-ton SS *Fort Babine* off the Portuguese coast, which was being towed to England for repair after being damaged by an earlier air attack in the Mediterranean. Although bombing accuracy was not good enough to score a direct hit, near-misses caused enough flooding for the crew to abandon the hulk. This was the last victory scored by a Condor in the Battle of the Atlantic. On October 1, III/KG 40 committed all 18 operational Condors to shadow and attack convoy MKS 25 off Spain but due to bad weather, only three found the ships and they scored no hits. Thereafter, *Fliegerführer Atlantik* relied on He 177s for the anti-shipping role. Even the Condor's pre-eminent role in maritime reconnaissance began to diminish when

Fernaufklärungsgruppe 5 (FAGr 5) became operational on October 15 with three Ju 290 bombers. The Ju 290, developed from the Ju 90, the Condor's pre-war competitor in the civil airline market, was now operational and it was far superior in the reconnaissance role to the Fw 200.

Although it was apparent that the Condor could no longer compete effectively on the battlefield of 1943, the Luftwaffe still had one card left to play. The Hs-293 guided bomb had been introduced with the Do 217s of II/KG 40 in August 1943 and several of the late-model Fw 200 C-6s in III/KG 40 were now being converted to launch this new weapon. Until they were ready, the He 177 was used in their stead. *Fliegerführer Atlantik* decided to send 25 He 177s from II/KG 40 against convoy MKS 30 on November 21, hoping to achieve a major success with a massed attack. The He 177s launched a total of 40 Hs-293s against the convoy but only sank one freighter and damaged another at the cost of three He 177s lost. On November 26, II/KG 40 tried another mission against a convoy sighted off Algeria and succeeded in hitting the troopship *Rohna* with an Hs-293. *Rohna* sank with the loss of 1,138 lives – mostly US Army troops. Although this attack successfully demonstrated the potential of the Hs-293 in standoff attacks, even the He 177 proved vulnerable to interception and II/KG 40 lost 12 of its 47 He 177s in November 1943.

A few Fw 200 C-6s were finally ready to participate in Hs-293 attacks just before the end of the year and one took off to bomb a convoy on December 28. However, the Condor was intercepted by a Short Sunderland while over the Bay of Biscay and after a short battle, the damaged Condor was forced to ditch. A few more Condor sorties were made in early 1944 but these slow and vulnerable aircraft could no longer get close enough to a convoy to launch the Hs-293.

AFTERMATH

By January 1944, II/KG 40 was reduced to only a handful of operational Fw 200s and it no longer posed a serious threat to Allied shipping. Nevertheless, a few Condors continued to be sent out on occasional maritime sorties even though these were close to becoming suicide missions. Still operating from Trondheim with a handful of Condors, 3./KG 40 sent three aircraft against convoy JW 58 heading to Murmansk on March 31, 1944. British convoy defenses were now firmly in place and JW 58 had air cover from the escort carriers HMS *Activity* and HMS *Tracker*. The Wildcat fighters from 819 Squadron easily splashed all three Condors, including one of the latest C-8 models. This mission proved to be the last serious Condor effort against a convoy but it was more of an execution than a duel. By this point, not only was the Fw 200 obsolete, but the OKL was cutting off production resources and aircrew training for all of its maritime units in favor of fighter production, effectively strangling the Condor's successors, the Ju 290 and He 177. Most of the remaining Condors spent the rest of the war as transports, reverting to their original role.

STATISTICS AND ANALYSIS

During the period June 1940 to September 1943, the Fw 200s of KG 40 sank a total of 93 ships of 433,447 tons and damaged a further 70 ships of 353,752 tons. As a percentage of total Allied merchant tonnage sunk by all Luftwaffe and Kriegsmarine forces, the contributions of KG 40 were minor; in 1940 they accounted for only 2.8 percent of all British tonnage sunk, rising to 5.4 percent in 1941, and diminishing to 2.5 percent in 1943. Compared to U-boats, the Fw 200 Condors were just a small, albeit sometimes helpful, adjunct. Even compared to other Luftwaffe anti-shipping units such as KG 26 and KG 30, the Condors accounted for less than one-quarter of all Allied merchant tonnage sunk by German air attacks. Given the relative handful of Fw 200s available in 1940–43, they did inflict a disproportionate share of damage compared to their shorter-ranged counterparts, the He 111s and Ju 88s, but this was mainly due to their striking a few large targets such as the *Empress of Britain* and *Duchess of York*.

Despite its impressive range, the Condor had a very limited bombload and poor ability to actually find convoys until it received the Hohentwiel radar in 1943. Condor anti-shipping operations only inflicted serious damage on six convoys: OB 290, HG 53, OB 287, SL 61, SL 62, and "Faith." All but one of these operations occurred during the high-water mark period for the Condor in January and February 1941. During the same year, KG 40 successfully attacked 15 convoys. To put their relative contribution into perspective, 29 HG-series convoys with a total of 584 ships ran from Gibraltar in 1941; of these convoys, only three were attacked by KG 40, resulting in seven ships being sunk. U-boats sank another 19 ships from the HG convoys in the same period. Against the 85 OB-series convoys with 3,061 ships in 1941, KG 40

An Fw 200 C-5 that crash-landed in Spain after a battle with a USAAF B-24D bomber on August 13, 1943. Note that the tail has snapped off. As usual, the Spanish allowed the German crewmen to return to France but the Condor was a write-off. (Author's collection)

attacked only six and sank 15 ships, while U-boats sank a further 16 ships. Finally, of the 49 SL-series convoys with 1,198 ships from Freetown, KG 40 attacked only four and sank eight ships, compared with 40 sunk by other German forces in 1941. Taken together, these statistics indicate that in their best year Condor anti-shipping operations only affected about one in ten convoys sailing in British waters and sank fewer than one out of every 100 ships in these convoys.

While the actual physical damage accomplished by the Fw 200s was fairly minor, the psychological impact of successful air attacks in areas where the British did not expect them – west of Ireland and off the Portuguese coast – was such as to cause the Admiralty great anxiety. The vulnerability of convoys to the low-level attacks of the Fw 200 in 1940 was particularly unnerving to the British, and following the sinking

The wreckage of an Fw 200 Condor shot down near a convoy in 1943. Survivors were rescued from this aircraft. By 1943, convoy defenses were so strong that the Condors could no longer achieve their former success. (Imperial War Museum AX 91A)

of the *Empress of Britain*, Churchill became actively involved. German propaganda, which greatly exaggerated the success of the Condor attacks, further pushed Churchill to demand immediate action to counteract the threat posed by KG 40. Churchill, given the feebleness of Britain's overall military position in the winter of 1940–41 and his inclination to strike back whenever possible, pushed both the Admiralty and the RAF to devote disproportionate resources to deal with the Condor threat. Indeed it could be claimed that the Condors won a "consolation" victory of sorts in pushing the British to expend resources on defensive armament, rather than offensive equipment such as bombers or landing craft.

By way of comparison, British defenses against the Condor in the period 1940–43 saw 45 Condors destroyed in the air and on the ground, although flak and fighter damage probably contributed to the loss of a number of other Fw 200s over water. Surprisingly, the biggest eliminator of Condors was anti-aircraft fire from the ubiquitous DEMS ships, which destroyed nine Fw 200s. In comparison, AA fire from Allied warships escorting the convoys only shot down four Condors with any certainty. FAA fighters from escort carriers claimed five Condors in 1941–43 and RAF fighters from CAM ships claimed another three. The 35 CAM ships proved to be a wasteful diversion of resources (accounting for the equivalent of two full RAF Hurricane squadrons), simply to provide a single-shot burst of air cover for a convoy. Land-based aircraft succeeded in intercepting at least 15 Condors, including eight by RAF Coastal Command and seven by the USAAF. In 1940, British convoy defenses were unable to shoot down any Condors but by 1941 about half the convoys that were attacked were able to damage or shoot down at least one Fw 200.

In addition to the attrition caused by British defenses, KG 40's operational effectiveness was undermined by the inherent poor suitability of the Fw 200 for the anti-shipping mission. Compared with other aircraft involved in such operations, such as the He 111H, Ju 88 and Do 217E, the Fw 200 had a very low operational readiness rate – often as low as 25 percent. It also suffered from a very high level of non-combat losses, at 52 percent, compared to 35–38 percent for all aircraft losses typically suffered by the seven other bomber *gruppen* supporting *Fliegerführer Atlantik*.

The final version of the Condor, the Fw 200 C-8, could carry two Hs-293 guided bombs. However, by the time that it was operational in December 1943 the Condor was too vulnerable to remain in front-line service. (Author's collection)

An Fw 200 Condor that has broken its back after a hard landing. Ultimately, the Condor proved to be a very fragile weapon and the fact that it suffered a very high accident rate meant that the Luftwaffe could never operate it in sufficient numbers to exert a decisive influence upon the Battle of the Atlantic. (Author's collection)

In addition to a significant number of crashes during take-off and landing, many Condors simply disappeared over the Atlantic, indicating a propensity for catastrophic failure. Most of the early Fw 200 C-1 and C-2 models were quickly debilitated by fuselage cracks, caused by their inability to handle large bomb loads and by low-level evasive maneuvering. In combat, the Fw 200 proved to have a "glass jaw" due to its lack of armored protection and inability to withstand being hit. Unlike other Luftwaffe bombers that could stagger back to base with significant damage, few damaged Condors made it back to Bordeaux.

In determining which factors were most important in deciding the outcome of the duel between the Condors and the Atlantic convoys, it is important to weigh each side's tactical ability and strategic choices made. Initially, the Luftwaffe showed itself as innovative and highly adaptable – mostly due to the efforts of a few junior officers – in converting the Fw 200 to the anti-shipping mission and developing effective low-level tactics for this jury-rigged bomber. German tactical prowess was enhanced by the poor strategic choices made by the Royal Navy prior to the war when it failed to devote adequate attention or resources to air defenses. The result was that the duel began in 1940–41 in lopsided favor of the Germans, at which time the Condor secured its reputation as "the scourge of the Atlantic." However, when Churchill energized the Admiralty and the RAF leadership to deal with the Condor threat, Britain compensated for its pre-war parsimony by indulging in a variety of *ad hoc* solutions. Once the Admiralty recognized the vulnerability of convoys to enemy air attack, it demonstrated great technical adaptability in converting freighters into CAM ships and escort carriers, as well as tactical ability in developing new procedures that increased the effectiveness of each convoy's AA fire. It was these British technical and tactical changes that quickly made Condor low-level attacks unprofitable by the fall of 1941.

Just when the duel seemed decided in Britain's favor by 1942, junior Luftwaffe leadership again showed great tactical adaptability in switching to medium-altitude bombing methods. The British were caught temporarily unprepared by this change of strategy, once more putting the outcome of the duel in doubt. German technical improvements, including Fw 200 models sporting Lotfe 7D bombsights and Hohentwiel radar, had the potential to restore the advantage to the offense. However, improvements in British inter-service coordination resulted in RAF Coastal Command providing the kind of air cover over convoys by 1943 that had only been dreamed about in 1940. Convoys with even modest air cover proved virtually immune to Condor attacks and ultimately, German tactical adaptability was starved of resources. This was due to both the failure of the Kriegsmarine and the Luftwaffe to work together effectively, and the failure of the RLM to prioritize the construction of suitable aircraft, in sufficient numbers, to attack more than a handful of British convoys. Furthermore, the Germans were willing to divert Condors to other missions – such as the attack on the Suez Canal and the Stalingrad airlift – rather than focus the limited number of their unique weapons system on just one achievable task. Amazingly, the RLM actually continued to divert some new-build Fw 200s for Lufthansa passenger use throughout the war. Seen in this light, the duel between the Condors and the Atlantic convoys was probably decided by the strategic choices each side made in allocating its resources during 1941, with Germany choosing to let *Fliegerführer Atlantik* conduct a shoestring aerial campaign against a tough, resourceful enemy that gradually regained its balance.

Condor victories and losses

Year	Sunk	Damaged	Fw 200s Destroyed by Allies	Other Fw 200 losses
1940	20 ships 114,044 GRT	37 ships 180,000 GRT	5	9
1941	58 ships 234,443 GRT	21 ships 112,256 GRT	14	21
1942	4 ships 2,629 GRT	1 ship 1,268 GRT	8	24
1943	11 ships 82,331 GRT	11 ships 60,228 GRT	18	34
TOTAL	*93 ships 433,447 GRT*	*70 ships 353,752 GRT*	*45*	*88*

Condor losses by cause

Year	AA from RN warship	AA from land / merchant ship	RAF in air / on ground	By FAA or CAM	By USAAF
1940	0	0/1	2/2	0	0
1941	1	4/0	2/3	4	0
1942	1	3/0	1/0	1	2
1943	2	2/0	6/0	3	5
TOTAL	*4*	*9/1*	*11/5*	*8*	*7*

CONCLUSION

British convoy defenses were initially based on misplaced faith that the RAF would protect any convoys within range of most German bombers and that the enemy would not be able to conduct effective anti-shipping strikes more than 1,000km from shore. The conversion of the Fw 200 Condor to the long-range anti-shipping role confounded this smug optimism and inflicted some embarrassing one-sided victories until the British realized their mistakes. Once the British began to rectify matters and commit significant resources to convoy defense, the Condor's dominance of the battle evaporated rather quickly.

Although the British won the duel between Condors and their Atlantic convoys, many of the lessons learned about protecting ships against air attack were forgotten in the post-war period, as was seen during the 1982 Falklands War when the Royal Navy had to fend off low-level air attacks once again. By that time, and due to exaggerated faith placed in missile defenses (not unlike the faith placed in the RAF to protect shipping in the 1930s), the rows of dependable 20mm Oerlikon and 40mm Bofors had been stripped from most ships, leaving them almost defenseless when the high-tech weapons failed to perform properly. An embarrassing number of ships were sunk off the Falklands by low-level attacks reminiscent of 1940–41. The *Fuerza Aerea Argentina* even resurrected the Fw 200 Condor concept by using three Boeing 707 airliners for long-range maritime reconnaissance, one of which spotted the British task force on April 21, 1982. In all likelihood, the history of warfare has probably not yet seen the last use of civilian aircraft for maritime reconnaissance and anti-shipping operations, or the need to protect merchant shipping from aerial attacks by *ad hoc* means.

FURTHER READING

Barker, Ralph, *Hurricats: The Fighters That Could Not Return*, Stroud,
    Tempus Publishing (2000)
Bowman, Martin, *B-24 Liberator 1939–45*, Wellingborough, Patrick Stephens (1979)
Brown, Eric, *Wings on My Sleeve*, London, Orion (2006)
Goss, Chris, *Sea Eagles: Luftwaffe Anti-Shipping Units,* Vols 1 & 2, Hersham,
    Ian Allan Publishing (2005–6)
Gould, Winston A., *Luftwaffe Maritime Operations in World War II: Thought,
    Organization and Technology*, USAF Air Command and Staff College (2005)
Hague, Arnold, *The Allied Convoy System 1939–1945*, St. Catharines, Canada,
    Vanwell Publishing (2000)
Hobbes, Commander David, RN, *Royal Navy Escort Carriers*, Liskeard,
    Maritime Books (2003)
McNeill, Ross, *RAF Coastal Command Losses*, Vol. 1, Hinckley,
    Midland Publishing (2003)
Murawski, Marek J., *Fw 200 Condor*, Lublin, Kagero (2007)
Neitzel, Sönke, "Kriegsmarine and Luftwaffe Co-operation in the War against
    Britain, 1939–1945," in *War in History*, Vol. 10, No. 4, pp. 448–463 (2003)
Nowarra, Heinz J., *Focke-Wulf Fw 200 "Condor,"* Koblenz, Bernard & Graefe (1988)
Spick, Mike, *Luftwaffe Bomber Aces*, London, Greenhill Books (2001)

Websites:

www.convoyweb.com
www.uboat.net

GLOSSARY

AA	anti-aircraft
AAMG	anti-aircraft machine gun
AMC	Armed Merchant Cruisers
AP-T	armor piercing tracer
ASDIC	submarine detection device
AVG	Auxiliary Aircraft Carriers
B-Dienst	German naval intelligence service
Bordfunker	radio operator
Bordmechaniker	aerial mechanic
Bordschuetz	aerial gunner
CAMS	Catapult Aircraft Merchant Ships
DEMS	Defensively Equipped Merchant Ships
Enigma	type of cipher encryption machine
FCS	Fighter Catapult Ships
Feldwebel	NCO rank equivalent to warrant officer
Fernaufklärungsgruppe 5	(*FAGr 5*) A special long-range reconnaissance group
Fernaufklärungstaffel	long-range reconnaissance squadron
Flieger	flyers
Fliegerkorps	air corps
Fliegerführer Atlantik	organization set up by Göring to conduct a coherent anti-shipping strategy in the Atlantic
Fliegerstaffel des Fuhrers	Hitler's personal squadron
Flugzeugführer	pilot
Generalstab	General Staff
Geschwaderkommodore	Luftwaffe rank, equivalent to a group commander, RAF

GIUK Gap	Greenland, Iceland, UK Gap area
Gruppe	group containing three or four *Staffel*
HA	high-angle
HEI-T	high-explosive incendiary tracer
Kampflieger	combat pilots
KG 40	*Kampfgeschwader* 40, German bomber force; within the KG 40 were *gruppen* (denoted by roman numerals, e.g. I/KG 40) overseeing *staffeln* (denoted by ordinals, e.g. 1./KG 40)
Kriegsmarine	German Navy during World War II
Luftlotte	German: air fleet
Luftwaffe	German Air Force
MSFU	Merchant Ship Fighter Unit
Obergefreiter	German rank equivalent to lance-corporal
OKL	*Oberkommando der Luftwaffe*, Air Force (Luftwaffe) High Command
OKW	*Oberkommando der Wehrmacht*, High Command of the German Armed Forces
Q-ship	decoy vessel
RLM	*Reichsluftfahrtsministerium*, Reich Air Ministry
Reichsmark (RM)	German currency 1924–1948
Ritterkreuz	Knight's Cross
SIGINT	Signals Intelligence
Staffel	Luftwaffe unit roughly equivalent to a squadron (plural – *staffeln*)
Tiefangriff	low-level attack tactics
unteroffizier	non-commissioned officer, roughly equivalent to corporal
USAAF	United States Army Air Force
Y-Service	monitors enemy radio transmissions

INDEX

References to illustrations are shown in **bold**. Plates are prefixed pl, with captions on the page in (brackets).